KINGFISHER First ENCYCLOPEDIA

KINGFISHER

NEW YORK

Cover Design Mike Yuen

Writers Anne Civardi, Ruth Thomson

General Consultant Margaret Mallet Ph.D.

U.S. Consultant Tom Schiele M.A.

Specialist Consultants
Michael Chinery B.Sc. (Natural Sciences)
Keith Lye B.A. F.R.G.S. (Geography)
Peter Mellett B.Sc. (Science and Technology)
James Muirden B.Ed. (Astronomy)
Dr. Elizabeth McCall Smith M.B. Ch.B.
    M.R.C.G.P. D.R.C.O.G. (Human Body)
Julia Stanton B.A. Dip.Ed. (Australasia)
Philip Steele B.A. (History and the Arts)
Dr. David Unwin B.Sc. Ph.D. (Paleontology)

KINGFISHER
LONDON & NEW YORK

Copyright © Kingfisher 2011
Published in the United States by Kingfisher,
175 Fifth Ave., New York, NY 10010
Kingfisher is an imprint of Macmillan Children's Books, London.

First published in 1996 by Kingfisher
This updated edition published in 2011 by Kingfisher

Distributed in the U.S. by Macmillan, 175 Fifth Ave., New York, NY 10010

Library of Congress Cataloging-in-Publication data has been applied for.

ISBN: 978-0-7534-6587-5

Kingfisher books are available for special promotions
and premiums. For details contact: Special Markets Department,
Macmillan, 175 Fifth Ave., New York, NY 10010.

For more information, please visit www.kingfisherbooks.com

Printed in China
2 4 6 8 9 7 5 3 1
1TR/0411/WKT/PICA/140MA

Your book

Your *First Encyclopedia* is packed with exciting information, amazing facts, and colorful pictures. All the topics appear in the order of the alphabet—a, b, c, and so on—and are listed on the next two pages. This page will show you how to use your book.

string puppets

◁ Information is written above, below, or next to each picture. Use the arrows to find out which picture to look at.

▷Look out for the numbered pictures. The numbers will help you look at the pictures in the right order.

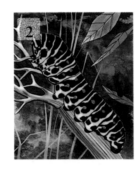

Fact box

These boxes tell you important things about each topic, including
• how big?
• how heavy?
• how long or wide?
• when did it happen?

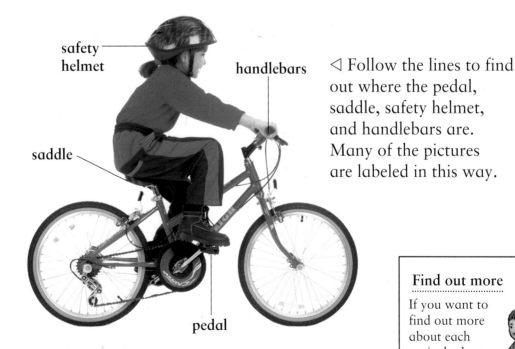

safety helmet

handlebars

saddle

pedal

◁ Follow the lines to find out where the pedal, saddle, safety helmet, and handlebars are. Many of the pictures are labeled in this way.

Find out more

If you want to find out more about each topic, look at this box. The list will show you which pages to look at.

◁ When you see these children, turn to the next page for more information on the same topic.

Contents

Africa

Africa is the second-largest and the warmest continent in the world. It has hot deserts, dense rainforests, and flat grasslands where many animals live. Many different peoples live in Africa. Most Africans live in the countryside and are farmers, but more and more are moving to the cities to find work.

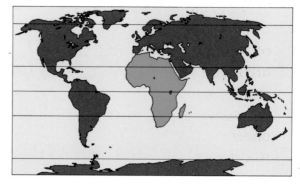

△ On this map Africa is shown in red. Africa is joined to Asia, and the Mediterranean Sea separates it from Europe.

▽ This man sells water to thirsty people who pass by. Water is very valuable in the desert.

◁ The Sahara covers almost one third of Africa. It is the world's biggest desert. It has the highest sand dunes in the world.

△ Cairo is the capital city of Egypt. It is also the largest city in Africa. It is located on the edge of the desert.

▷ In many villages, women share the work of preparing meals together. Here they are pounding grain into flour to make pancakes.

▷ Diamonds from the country of South Africa are found by miners who dig thousands of feet under the ground to get them.

▷ This beautiful bottle is made out of a gourd, a plant like a pumpkin. It was made in Kenya and has a stopper shaped like a human head.

▷ Africa's large grasslands are home to many animals, such as these elephants. People now use the grasslands for their herds of cattle, too.

△ Maputo is the capital city of Mozambique in southeast Africa. It is a modern city with many skyscrapers. It is also a busy port.

Find out more

Art and artists
Grasslands
History
Water
World

Air

Air is all around you. It has no shape. It goes in all directions and fills every bit of space. Air is made up of things called gases. Gases are invisible. You cannot see, smell, or taste them. One of these gases is called oxygen. People and animals need to breathe in oxygen to stay alive.

parachute

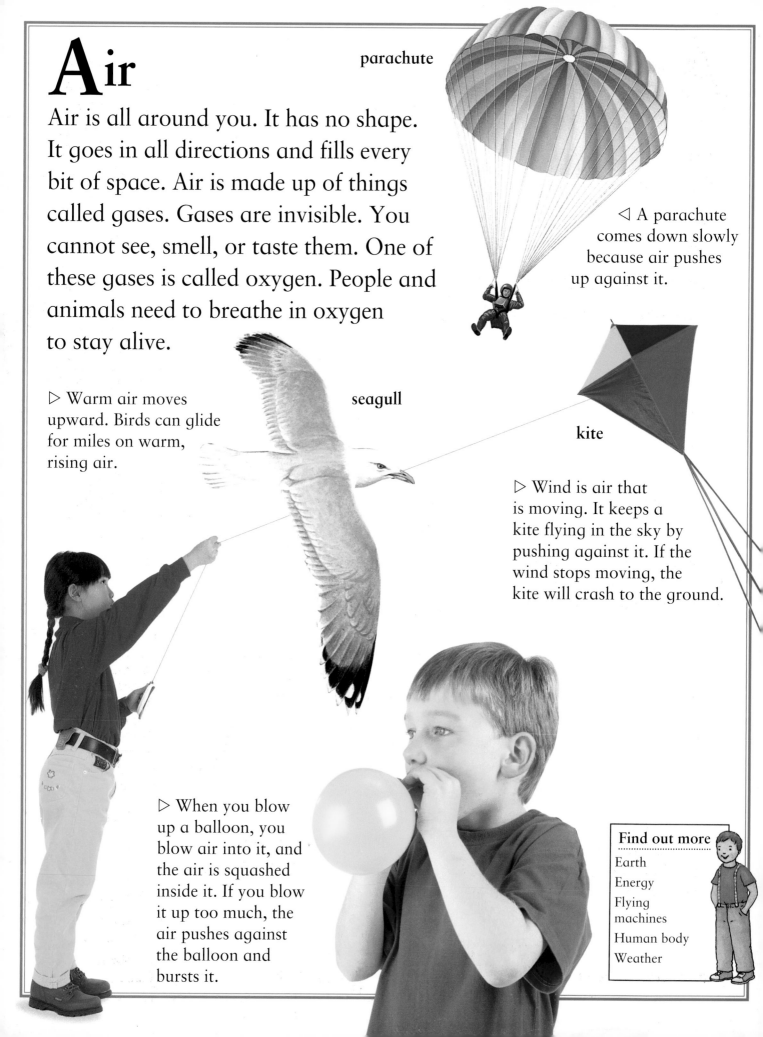

◁ A parachute comes down slowly because air pushes up against it.

▷ Warm air moves upward. Birds can glide for miles on warm, rising air.

seagull

kite

▷ Wind is air that is moving. It keeps a kite flying in the sky by pushing against it. If the wind stops moving, the kite will crash to the ground.

▷ When you blow up a balloon, you blow air into it, and the air is squashed inside it. If you blow it up too much, the air pushes against the balloon and bursts it.

Find out more
Earth
Energy
Flying machines
Human body
Weather

Amphibians

Frogs, toads, salamanders, and newts are all amphibians. Most amphibians are born in water. As they grow, they change so that they can also live on land. The largest amphibian is the Japanese giant salamander, which can grow up to 5 feet (1.5m) long.

◁ A frog has smooth, slimy skin. It leaps by pushing hard with its long back legs.

frog

△ 1 In the spring, female frogs lay their eggs in water. 2 The eggs hatch into tadpoles with wriggly tails.

▷ A toad has a fat body with rough, dry skin. It has no tail. It often lives in drier places than a frog.

toad

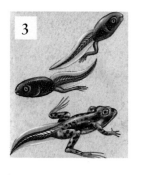

△ The tadpoles grow fatter, and their legs appear. 4 Once they lose their tails, the frogs can leave the water to look for food.

▽ Most salamanders and newts lay eggs in water. They grow in the same way as frogs and toads, but they do not lose their tails.

long-tailed salamander

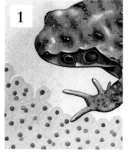

Fact box

• An amphibian is cold-blooded. This means that its body is always the same temperature as the air or water around it.

• Amphibians have backbones, so they are called vertebrates.

great crested newt

Find out more
Animals
Prehistoric life
Water

Animals

Animals are living things that get their energy to move and grow by eating food. They are all shapes and sizes—from huge whales to animals so tiny that thousands would fit on a teaspoon. Some animals even live inside other animals and plants. Animals can be found all over the world—in hot, dry deserts, in icy oceans, and on freezing cold mountaintops.

△ This animal is so small that it can be seen only through a microscope.

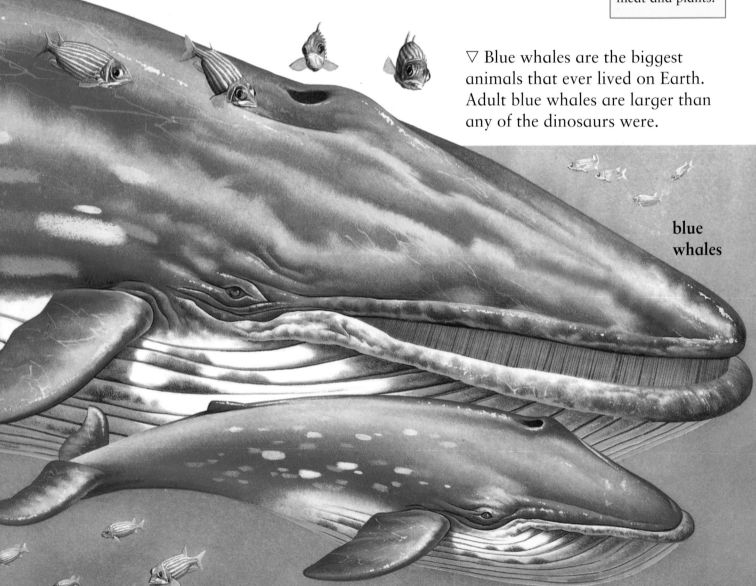

▽ Blue whales are the biggest animals that ever lived on Earth. Adult blue whales are larger than any of the dinosaurs were.

blue whales

Animals in air

Most animals that have wings can fly. Moths and bats usually fly around at night. Falcons and most other birds fly in the daytime to find food. Falcons swoop down to catch prey.

moth

falcon

long-eared bat

Animals on land

Stocky wombats move slowly. They go into underground burrows if they are scared. Zebras are able to gallop away from danger. Snakes can slither quickly across the ground.

coral snake

wombats

zebra

Animals in water

Jellyfish pump water through their bodies to push themselves along. Crabs scuttle sideways across the ocean floor. Fish swim by moving their tails from side to side.

jellyfish

angelfish

crab

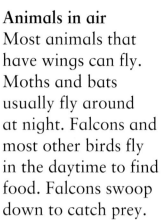

Vertebrates

Animals that have a backbone are called vertebrates.

gila monster

△ **Reptiles** are cold-blooded. They need heat from the sun to stay warm.

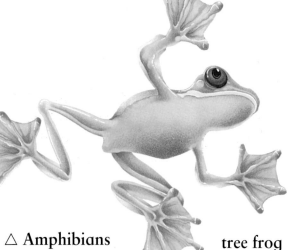

△ **Amphibians** can live in the water and on land. They usually lay their eggs in water but spend most of their time on land.

tree frog

stickleback

monkey

△ **Mammals** usually have hair or fur to keep them warm. Babies are cared for by their mothers and feed on their mothers' milk.

△ **Fish** live in water. They breathe with gills, which are slits just behind their heads. Their bodies are covered in tiny scales.

hummingbird

◁ **Birds** are covered with feathers and also have wings. Most birds can fly. All birds have beaks, or bills, instead of teeth.

Invertebrates

Animals without backbones are called invertebrates.

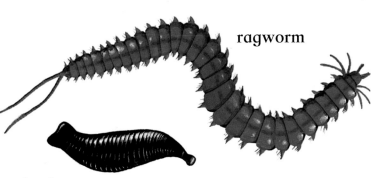

ragworm

leech

△ **Worms** have long, thin, soft bodies with no legs. Their bodies are made up of many small sections.

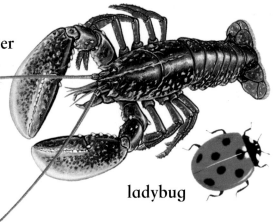

lobster

ladybug

△ These animals have tough outer skins to protect their soft bodies. Their legs are jointed, like a suit of armor, so that they can move.

▷ These **jellylike animals** live in the ocean. They have stinging tentacles for catching food and for protection.

Portuguese man-of-war

sea anemone

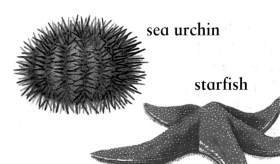

sea urchin

starfish

△ Some **spiny-skinned animals** live on the ocean floor. They move around on tube feet, which have suckers on the ends.

▷ **Soft-bodied animals** need to keep their bodies moist, so many of them live in water. Some of them have a hard shell to protect their soft bodies.

snail

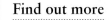

octopus

Find out more

Amphibians
Birds
Camouflage
Conservation
Dinosaurs
Fish
Insects
Mammals
Prehistoric life
Reptiles
Spiders
Zoos

Antarctica and the Arctic

Antarctica and the Arctic are very cold places. They are found at opposite ends of Earth. Antarctica is in the south. It is the fifth-biggest continent and is completely covered by ice. It is the coldest place on Earth. The Arctic is in the north. Most of it is a frozen ocean. In the spring, some of its ice breaks up.

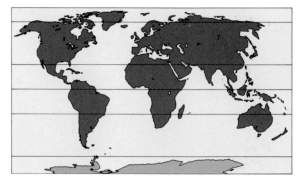

△ Antarctica is shown in green, and the Arctic is at the top of the map. They are Earth's coldest places.

▷ Roald Amundsen, a Norwegian explorer, and his team were the first people to reach the South Pole in Antarctica.

penguins

▽ Emperor penguins live in Antarctica. They hold their eggs and chicks on their feet to keep them warm.

polar bear

△ Bands of colored light often appear in the night skies of Antarctica and the Arctic. In the Arctic, they are called the aurora borealis, or northern lights. In Antarctica, they are called the aurora australis, or southern lights.

△ The polar bear lives in the Arctic. It is a strong swimmer and a good runner. It catches seals, fish, and birds with its strong paws and has a thick coat of hair to protect it from the cold.

△ Many scientists work in the Arctic and Antarctica. They record the weather, measure the depth of the ice, and study the wildlife.

△ During the winter in the Arctic and Antarctica, there are only a few hours of daylight. In the summer, the opposite happens, and the sun shines all night and day.

Find out more

World

Art and artists

Art is something beautiful made by a person. Painting, carving, pottery, and weaving are just a few types of art. Artists create art for many reasons. They may want to tell a story or record an event, a person, or a place. Sometimes artists create things for a magical or religious reason or just because they enjoy doing it.

△ The Aboriginal people of Australia painted rock or cave pictures thousands of years ago.

◁ The ancient Greeks painted scenes from everyday life on their pottery vases. This man is hunting deer.

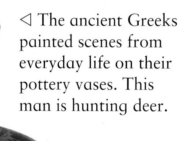

▷ Everyday things can also be art. This colorful cloth was made in Ghana, Africa, for clothing, but it is beautiful enough to be a work of art.

▷ Scenes from nature are popular art subjects in Japan. This beautiful print of a stormy sea was made by a Japanese artist named Hokusai.

▽ This Polynesian sculptor is carving a stone figure called a tiki. He uses a hammer and sharp chisel to carve out the image.

▷ Edgar Degas, a French artist, was very interested in showing how dancers moved. He painted many pictures of ballet dancers.

◁ The painter Jackson Pollock laid his canvases on the floor. Then he dripped, threw, or poured paint all over them to make swirling shapes and patterns.

Find out more

Africa
Books
Color
Stories

Asia

Asia is the biggest continent. It has large forests, deserts, and grasslands. It has many high mountains and some very long rivers. More than half of the world's people live in Asia. Many are farmers. Others live in large, busy cities. Very few people live in the deserts or the rocky mountain areas.

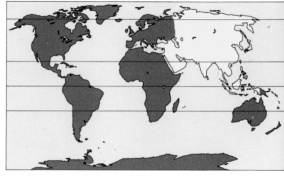

△ Asia is shown in yellow on this map. It includes almost one third of all the land on Earth.

▽ Camels carry people and goods across the desert. They are also raced in the desert country of Saudi Arabia.

△ Rice is grown in the warm, wet parts of Asia. It is usually grown in fields cut into a mountainside. The low-walled fields, called terraces, are flooded with water.

◁ Kyrgyz (kir-**geez**) girls and women wear colorful clothes. Kyrgyzstan is in western Asia. The people herd sheep in the winter and farm in the summer.

◁ Shanghai is the biggest city in China. It is busy and very crowded. New skyscrapers are being built to provide homes.

△ The tea ceremony is a very old and popular tradition in Japan. The tea is made and drunk very slowly and carefully.

◁ The highest mountains in the world are in the Himalayas, between India and China. The highest of all is Mount Everest.

▽ Every July, at the full moon, richly decorated elephants parade with dancers and drummers through the streets of Kandy in Sri Lanka.

Find out more

Dance
Drama
Farming
Religion
World

19

Australia and the Pacific Islands

Australia is a country and the world's smallest continent. Most people live in cities along the coasts. Away from the coasts the land is called the bush and the outback. The Pacific is the world's largest and deepest ocean. It has many small islands. The Pacific Islands, Australia, and New Zealand together make up Oceania.

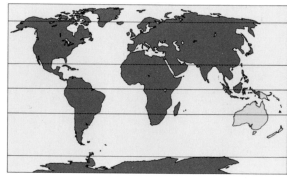

△ Australia, New Zealand, and the many islands of the Pacific Ocean are shown in orange on this map.

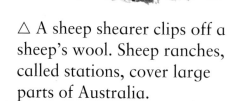

▽ Many Pacific islands are surrounded by coral reefs. Many types of brightly colored fish live in the warm waters of the reefs.

△ A sheep shearer clips off a sheep's wool. Sheep ranches, called stations, cover large parts of Australia.

▷ These musicians are Aboriginal people. Their ancestors were the first people to settle in Australia, a long time ago.

▷ Sydney is the largest city in Australia. It is also Australia's oldest city. Its world-famous Opera House (on the left of this picture) overlooks the harbor.

Uluru (Ayers Rock)

▷ The koala is a marsupial. It sleeps all day and is awake at night. It is around 2 feet (30cm) long. It lives among the branches of eucalyptus trees, and the leaves of the eucalyptus are its main food supply. Its strong claws help it cling to tree trunks.

koalas

▽ On the North Island of New Zealand, there are many geysers, which are jets of boiling water and steam that burst high up into the air.

Find out more
Buildings
Farming
History
Stories
World

Babies

Very young children are called babies. A baby begins when a tiny egg inside its mother joins together with a tiny part of its father called a sperm. The baby grows inside its mother's uterus, where it is kept safe and warm. After about nine months, the baby is ready to be born.

sperm ——

egg

◁ This egg is surrounded by many sperm. Only one of the sperm will get inside the egg.

▷ A baby grows inside its mother's uterus. It gets all the food it needs through a tube called the umbilical cord.

umbilical cord

▽ A newborn baby needs a lot of care and attention. It must be fed, bathed, kept warm, and protected.

▷ Most babies start to walk without help between the ages of 12 and 18 months.

Find out more
Food
Human body
Mammals

Bikes

Bicycles, or bikes, and motorcycles are two-wheeled machines that you can use to travel around— much faster than you can walk. Bikes are fun to ride, and because they do not have engines, there is no fuel to pollute the air. Motorcycles have engines, and they can travel as fast as cars.

◁ This wooden bike was built more than 100 years ago.

▽ To ride a bike, you push the pedals. The pedals turn the chain. The chain moves the back wheel around. This makes the bike move.

handlebars

fuel tank

saddle

safety helmet

tailpipe

engine

△ The engine of a motorcycle makes the wheels go around. The engine runs on gasoline, which is stored in the fuel tank.

handlebars

brake lever

saddle

front reflector

back reflector

brake pad

pedal

chain

Find out more

Energy

Inventions

Machines

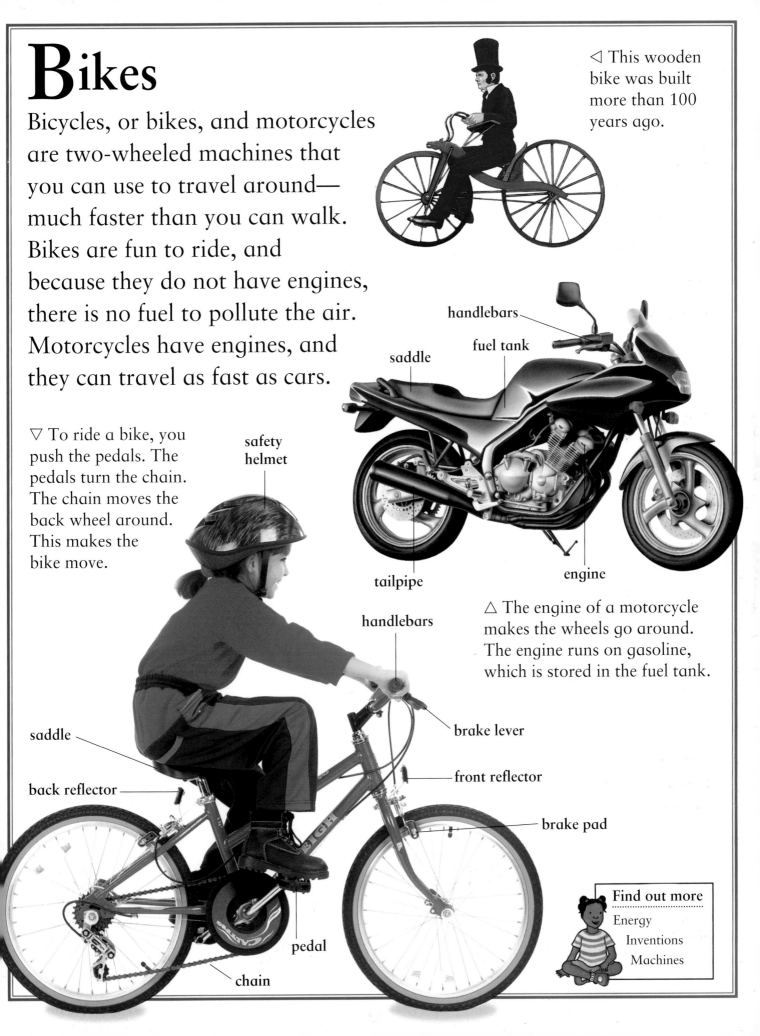

Birds

Birds are the only animals with feathers. They also have wings. There are thousands of different birds, in all shapes, sizes, and colors. The biggest bird is the ostrich. The smallest bird is the bee hummingbird, which is around 2 inches (5.5cm) long and weighs less than one tenth of an ounce.

tail feathers

eye

ear

beak

claw

wing

▷ Many male birds have colorful feathers to attract female birds. So a peacock shows off to a peahen.

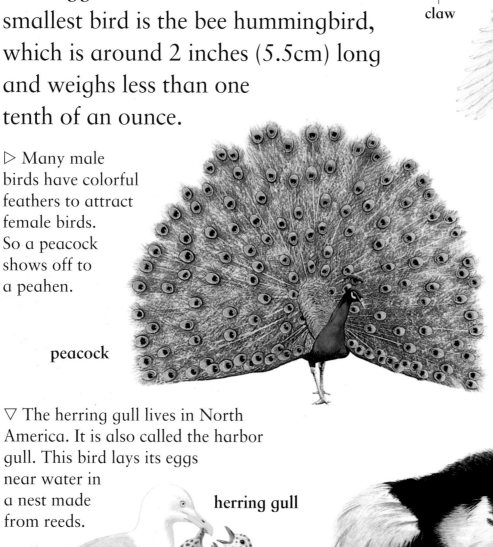

peacock

▽ An ostrich is around 8 feet (2.5m) tall and weighs 300 pounds (135kg). It is too heavy to fly but uses its strong legs to run very fast. An ostrich can run faster than a racehorse.

▽ The herring gull lives in North America. It is also called the harbor gull. This bird lays its eggs near water in a nest made from reeds.

herring gull

ostrich

wren

▷ A wren's beak is shaped for snatching insects. An avocet has a long, curved beak to scoop up small water animals. A toucan uses its big beak to push aside leaves in order to pick up fruit and nuts.

avocet

toucan

▽ Some birds are hunters. The eagle uses its sharp, hooked claws, called talons, to catch its prey.

eagle

talon

Canada geese

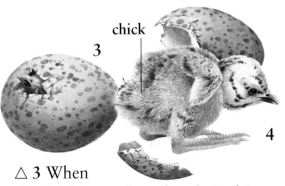

▷ In the fall, many birds migrate. This means that they fly to warmer places. They may fly thousands of miles. They return in the spring.

Fact box

• Birds have beaks, or bills, instead of teeth.

• All birds hatch from eggs. The eggs have hard shells. They are laid by female birds.

• Most birds can fly. Penguins are birds that cannot fly. They use their wings to swim.

• Many birds have some hollow bones that help make them light enough to fly.

embryo

1   2   3   chick   4

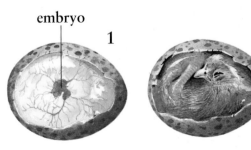

△ 1 Each bird's egg has an embryo. A chick develops from the embryo. 2 The shell protects the growing chick.

△ 3 When the chick is ready to hatch, it chips a hole in the eggshell. 4 Then the chick breaks out of the shell.

Find out more
Air
Animals
Antarctica and the Arctic
Conservation
Prehistoric life
Seashores

Books

The first books were rare and precious. They were written by hand, which took a long time. Then a machine called a printing press was invented. This made it possible to make many copies of each book. Today most books are made of paper and cardboard. They are printed on very fast machines.

scrolls

◁ The ancient Egyptians made some of the first books. They were written on scrolls made from a reed called papyrus.

▷ Long ago, monks copied books by hand. They decorated each page with colorful designs and pictures.

▽ This printing machine was built by Johannes Gutenberg, more than 500 years ago. The Bible was one of the first books he printed.

How a book is made

1

△ A team of people meet to plan the book. They decide on its size and what it will look like. Then it has to be written by an author.

2

△ When the author has written the words, an editor carefully reads them. The editor corrects any mistakes on a computer screen.

3

△ An illustrator draws pictures to go with the words. Sometimes a photographer takes photographs to put in the book, too.

4

△ The designer decides how to arrange the words and pictures on each page. She then puts the pages on a computer disk.

5

△ From the disk, film and printing plates are made. At the printer, a printing press prints the pages onto large sheets of paper.

6

△ The printed sheets are folded and cut into separate pages. They are sewn or glued together. Then a cover is put around the pages.

▷ You can use books to find out facts about animals, machines, history, or science. Other books have stories in them. Millions of books are made every year.

Find out more

Forests
History
Maps
Stories
Writing

Buildings

Buildings give us shelter in all types of weather. Houses are often made of whatever materials can be found easily. Buildings are all types of sizes and styles and are usually built for a special purpose. These include churches and temples, schools, office buildings, factories, movie theaters, and health clubs.

△ Buildings near woods are often made of logs. They have stone chimneys to keep fire away from the wooden walls.

▽ Bundles of reeds were used to build houses in the marshes of Iraq. Reed houses were still built by Marsh Arabs until recently.

△ Stone is heavy to move. So stone houses are usually built in areas where stone can be found nearby.

▽ In hot places such as Africa, many buildings are made of mud, baked hard by the sun. These buildings are cool and shady.

△ Many houses are made of brick. The bricks are joined with mortar, a mixture of water, sand, and cement.

Famous buildings

Leaning
Tower of
Pisa

Sydney Opera House

◁ The Sydney
Opera House in
Australia overlooks
a large harbor. Its
roof looks like the
sails of a boat.

◁ Italy's Leaning
Tower of Pisa was
built on soft ground.
Every year the tower
leans a tiny bit more.

▷This structure
at Epcot Center in
Florida's Walt Disney
World looks like
a giant golf ball.

Epcot
Center

◁ Skyscrapers
have a skeleton
made of steel.
Concrete floors,
outside walls,
and windows
are added when
the skeleton
is complete.

Find out more

Australia and
the Pacific
Islands
Castles
Religion
Sports

Camouflage

The colors and markings of some animals look like their surroundings. This is called camouflage. It makes the animals hard to spot. Camouflage helps animals hide from their enemies. It also helps them creep up on animals that they are hunting.

leaf insect

◁ This strange leaf insect has markings on its wings that look just like the veins of a leaf.

Arctic hare

tiger

◁ A tiger's coat has a pattern of dark and light stripes. This makes it hard to spot when it creeps through long grass toward an animal it is hunting.

△ Arctic hares are white to match the snow in the winter. In the summer, their fur turns brown.

△ A chameleon can change the color of its skin. This means it can hide in many different places.

▷ Camouflage fabric is made to help people hide. Bird watchers can see much more if the birds cannot spot them.

Find out more

Forests
Grasslands

Cars

There is a car for every purpose. Some are large enough to carry a family of six, a large dog, and supermarket supplies for a month. Sports cars are small and fast. Cars such as police cars are necessary for work. People should use cars and fuel that don't waste much energy or pollute the air.

Benz's Motorwagen

△ The first gasoline-driven car was invented by a German, Karl Benz. He put an engine into a horse cart.

windshield

engine

gas tank

axle

Formula 1 racecar

▽ A racecar has a powerful engine. Its wide wheels help the car stay firmly on the road when it is going fast.

△ A car has hundreds of different moving parts to make it go.

four-wheel drive

▷ A four-wheel drive vehicle is specially built so that it can be driven over rough or muddy ground.

Find out more
Computers
Conservation
Energy
Inventions
Machines
Roads

Castles

Most castles were built hundreds of years ago. They had high towers and thick walls that sheltered people from their enemies. The first castles were built of wood. Later they were built of stone. Castles often have deep ditches around them called moats.

motte

bailey

△ Wooden castles were built on a mound called a motte. People lived outside the castle in an area called a bailey. They went into the castle only when they were attacked.

▽ The armies of rival kings or lords used tall wooden towers, catapults, and battering rams to attack and break into other castles.

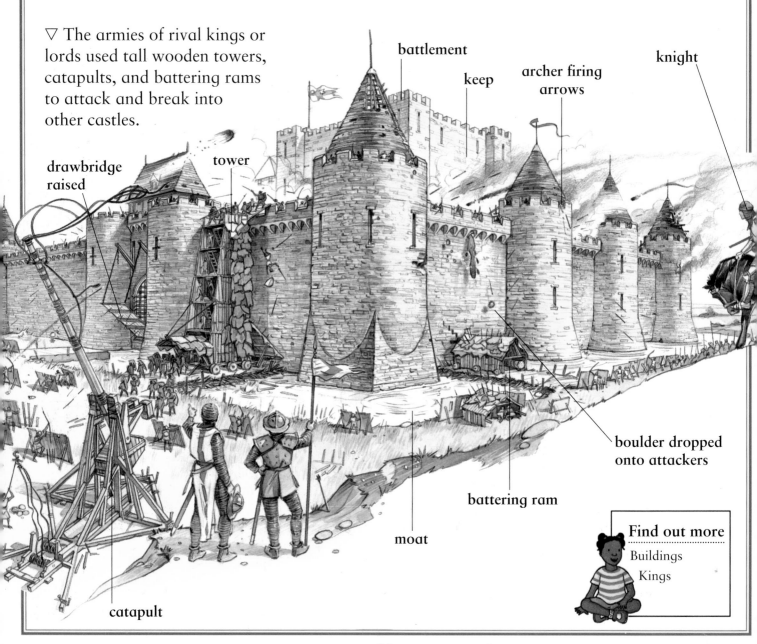

battlement

keep

archer firing arrows

knight

drawbridge raised

tower

boulder dropped onto attackers

battering ram

moat

catapult

Find out more

Buildings

Kings

Caves

Caves are big holes in rock. They are usually underground, dark, and damp. Most caves are formed by water. The largest caves in the world are found in rock called limestone. Ancient humans used big, dry caves to live in. Some modern people explore underground caves as a hobby. This is called caving or spelunking.

bats

△ Bats often live in caves. They sleep in them during the day and fly out to hunt at night. The caves are a safe home for young bats.

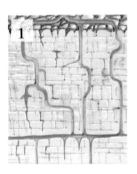

1

△ Water sinks into the cracks in limestone. It eats away at the rock and makes tunnels.

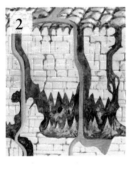

2

△ Over thousands of years, the tunnels get deeper and wider until they become big caves.

stalactite

column

stalagmite

▷ Water dripping from a cave roof has minerals in it. When the water dries, the minerals are left behind. They form stalactites and stalagmites. These can meet and form columns.

Find out more

Art
Earth
Mammals

Clothes

Clothes are the things we wear on our bodies. People wear different clothes to suit the jobs they do, the games they play, and the weather. In some jobs, people wear uniforms so that they are easy to recognize. Most clothes are made in factories.

Inuit child

◁ People who live in very cold places wear clothes that keep them warm and dry.

Tuareg man

▷ In hot, dry deserts, people wear long robes and scarves. This protects them from the heat of the sun.

▽ When the weather is wet and rainy, waterproof things help keep your clothes dry.

▽ Firefighters wear special clothes to protect them from heat and smoke.

firefighter

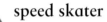

speed skater

◁ Clothes for sports must be light and easy to move around in. They are often made of tight, stretchy fabrics.

Find out more
Dance
Deserts
Drama
Space exploration
Sports

Color

Our world is full of colors. Without them, it would be a very dull place. Colors are very useful. Plants grow bright flowers to attract insects. We use red signs to warn people of danger.

You need light to see colors. During the day, you see many colors. At night, with no light, everything is black.

◁ A wasp has bright yellow stripes. These warn birds to stay away from its painful stinger.

wasp

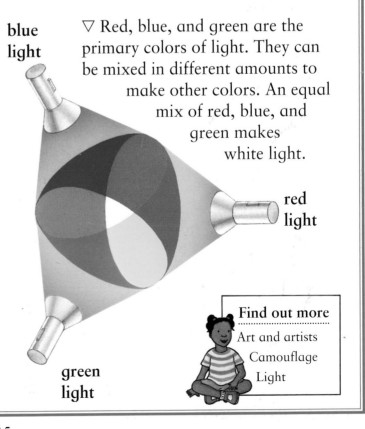

▷ Dyes are used to change the color of fabrics. You can make dyes from natural things such as plants, vegetables, and berries.

Yellow and blue make green.

Blue and red make purple.

Yellow and red make orange.

blue light

▽ Red, blue, and green are the primary colors of light. They can be mixed in different amounts to make other colors. An equal mix of red, blue, and green makes white light.

red light

green light

△ Primary colors are mixed to make other colors. Red, yellow, and blue are the primary colors of paint. They can make almost any color except white.

Find out more
Art and artists
Camouflage
Light

35

Computers

A computer is a machine that can store huge amounts of information. Computers contain parts called microchips to make them work, and people write programs to tell them what to do. Computers can solve difficult number problems very fast. Banks, stores, factories, and offices all use computers. You can also use them at home.

△ The Colossus, one of the earliest computers, was enormous. It helped decode enemy messages during World War II.

screen

keyboard

△ Car factories use computer-controlled robots to build cars. The robots weld the car parts together.

▷ This thin computer is an e-book reader— a device for reading electronic books. Lighter than a paperback, it can store a whole library of books.

◁ You can enter information into a computer using a keyboard and a mouse, a CD-ROM, or a USB memory stick. You can also search for information on the Internet. Words, pictures, and even movies can be displayed on the screen.

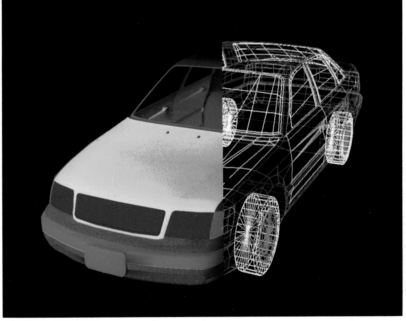

△ Car designers use computers to plan new cars. The computer can test out the designs to see if the new car will work on the road.

◁ Computers are also fun. You have to be quick to score well on a hand-held computer game.

Find out more
Books
Electricity
Jobs
Music
Space
exploration

Conservation

People hunt animals for their fur, horns, and meat. They dig up plants and flowers because they are beautiful, and they cut down trees for their wood. Some types of animals and plants have died out completely. We must protect our world and its wildlife. This is called conservation.

◁ The dodo became extinct more than 200 years ago.

dodo

rhinoceros

◁ If many more rhinos are killed for their horns, these animals will die out.

slipper orchid

▷ Some wild orchids are very rare, but people still dig them up.

◁ Forests are cut down for timber and to make room for roads, farms, and buildings. The animals who live in them are in danger because they can lose their homes and their food.

△ Factories cannot just dump their waste products anymore. They now have to protect the water and air.

△ Farmers use chemicals to help their crops. They are now trying to use chemicals that do not harm wild plants and animals.

△ Modern cars have been made so that they release less fumes. This is to reduce pollution of the air and soil.

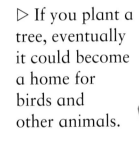

▷ If you plant a tree, eventually it could become a home for birds and other animals.

▷ A bird covered in oil accidentally spilled by a tanker will die unless it is carefully cleaned.

▷ You can help clean up your world by saving cardboard, paper, bottles, and cans to use again. This is called recycling.

Find out more
Energy
Farming
Forests
Plants
Zoos

Dance

ballet shoes

When you dance, you move your body in time to music. You may follow a pattern of steps or just twist and twirl and stamp your feet to fit the music. People all over the world love to dance. Many dancers use their hands and bodies to tell a story.

◁ This Indian dancer moves her hands and fingers in a special way. Her movements tell a story about the Hindu gods.

▷ Most ballet dancers first learn to dance when they are young. They learn special positions for their hands and feet.

◁ Spanish flamenco dancers stamp and tap their heels and toes. They move their hands while they twist and turn their bodies in time to guitar music.

▷ These Russian folk dancers jump high and kick out their legs to fast music.

Find out more
Art and artists
Asia
Europe
Music
Religion

40

Deserts

A desert is a dry place where little or no rain falls. Few people live there. Only tough plants and animals can live in these rocky or sandy places. Many deserts are blazing hot during the day and freezing cold at night. Some deserts are cold most of the time.

△ Monument Valley is in Arizona and Utah. Strong winds blow the sand around, and this has worn the rocks into strange shapes.

▷ These people are nomads. This means that they travel around to find food and water. They often live in tents that can be moved easily.

desert scorpion

△ The scorpion is a deadly hunter. It has a poisonous stinger in its tail.

◁ A camel can travel a long way without eating and drinking. It stores fat in its hump and uses this for food.

camel

prickly pear cactus

◁ Cactus plants store water in their thick stems. The spines protect the plants from being eaten by animals.

Find out more

Africa
Antarctica and the Arctic
Asia
North America
Plants

Dinosaurs

Dinosaurs lived on Earth millions of years ago. These scaly-skinned animals were all shapes and sizes. Some were huge creatures that weighed ten times as much as an elephant, while others were the size of chickens. Some were fierce meat eaters, and some ate only plants.

△ Scientists study fossils of dinosaur footprints. They can use them to figure out how dinosaurs moved and how fast they ran.

Fact box

• The word *dinosaur* means "terrible lizard."

• Dinosaurs lived on Earth long before the first human beings.

• Dinosaurs became extinct around 65 million years ago. We do not know why they died out.

◁ Dinosaurs laid eggs. *Maiasaura* laid eggs in a nest that she dug in the ground. She cared for her babies after they hatched.

Maiasaura
(**My**-a-**saw**-ra)

▷ This is the skeleton of *Tyrannosaurus rex*. It lived in North America. It was around 50 feet (15m) long and 20 feet (6.5m) tall. It weighed around 20 tons.

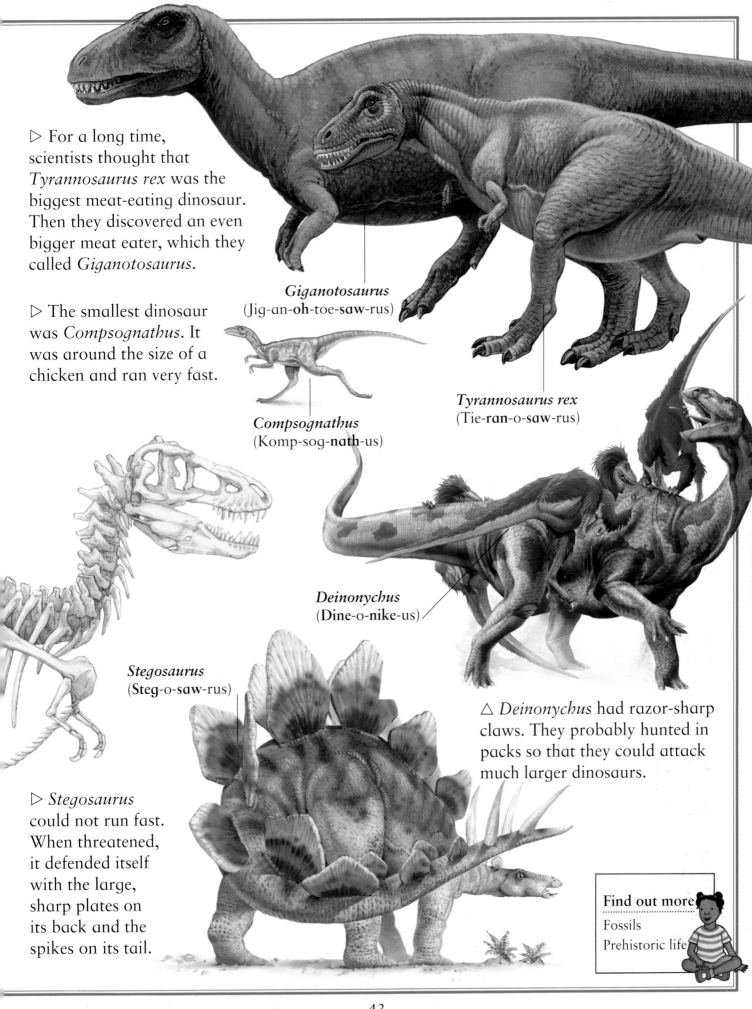

▷ For a long time, scientists thought that *Tyrannosaurus rex* was the biggest meat-eating dinosaur. Then they discovered an even bigger meat eater, which they called *Giganotosaurus*.

▷ The smallest dinosaur was *Compsognathus*. It was around the size of a chicken and ran very fast.

Giganotosaurus
(Jig-an-**oh**-toe-**saw**-rus)

Compsognathus
(Komp-sog-**nath**-us)

Tyrannosaurus rex
(Tie-**ran**-o-**saw**-rus)

Stegosaurus
(**Steg**-o-**saw**-rus)

Deinonychus
(Dine-o-**nike**-us)

△ *Deinonychus* had razor-sharp claws. They probably hunted in packs so that they could attack much larger dinosaurs.

▷ *Stegosaurus* could not run fast. When threatened, it defended itself with the large, sharp plates on its back and the spikes on its tail.

Find out more
Fossils
Prehistoric life

Drama

Drama is a story told in words and actions. Most dramas are called plays. They are performed by actors on a stage in front of an audience. Most plays are performed in a theater. You can also watch drama on television and in movies or listen to it on the radio.

◁ Puppets can be used instead of people to perform plays. These puppets are from India.

▷ You could put on your own play. Decide on a story and make some scenery. Dress up in costumes and put on makeup. Then ask people to come watch.

△ This woman is a mime. She uses her body instead of words to tell a story.

◁ Kabuki is a type of play performed in Japan. All the parts are played by men. They wear colorful costumes and lots of makeup.

Find out more

History

Jobs

Stories

44

Earth

Earth is our planet. It is a giant ball of rock spinning in space around the Sun. It is the only planet we know that has life. Earth gets the heat and light it needs from the Sun. A blanket of air called the atmosphere surrounds Earth. This is the air we breathe. Large areas of water cover most of Earth's surface. Without air and water, there would be no life on Earth.

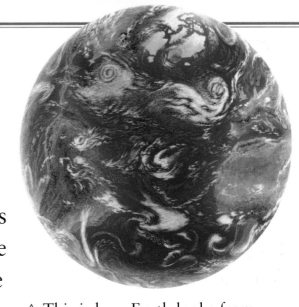

△ This is how Earth looks from space. Swirling white patterns are made by clouds in the atmosphere.

Sun

Earth

◁ It takes just over 365 days for Earth to travel around the Sun. This is one year on Earth.

▷ We have day and night because Earth turns as it travels around the Sun. Imagine that the flashlight is the Sun. The side facing it has daylight. The other side has night.

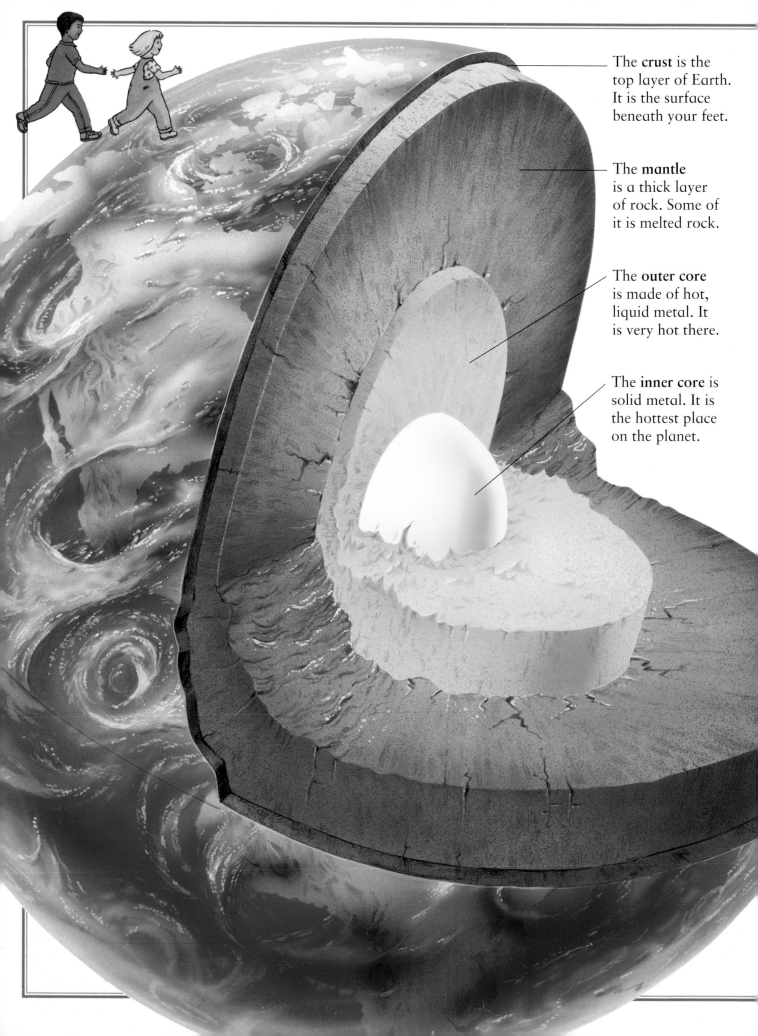

The **crust** is the top layer of Earth. It is the surface beneath your feet.

The **mantle** is a thick layer of rock. Some of it is melted rock.

The **outer core** is made of hot, liquid metal. It is very hot there.

The **inner core** is solid metal. It is the hottest place on the planet.

▽ The crust is made from many different types of rocks. Most are made deep inside Earth.

sandstone

marble

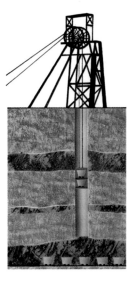

granite

limestone

amethyst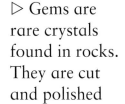

yellow sapphire

▷ Gems are rare crystals found in rocks. They are cut and polished to make jewels.

rock crystal

Fact box

• Water covers around three fourths of Earth.

• Earth was formed around 4.6 billion years ago from clouds of hot gas and dust.

• Earth measures about 25,000 miles (40,000km) around the middle.

△ Coal is made from the remains of plants that died millions of years ago. It is dug out of the ground by miners and used as fuel.

△ Miners drill for oil and gas on land and under the sea. They often work on huge rigs far out at sea.

▷ Earthquakes happen when parts of the crust push against each other or move apart. This makes the ground shake. Cracks appear in the ground, and buildings may collapse.

Find out more

Oceans and seas
Planets
Seasons
Sun
Volcanoes
Weather
World

Electricity

Electricity is a type of energy. It can move along wires. When it flows along a wire, this is called an electric current. Electricity is used to make heat, light, sound, and movement—it can make all types of machines work. Electricity can be stored in batteries, too.

△ You can make a type of electricity. Rub a balloon on a wool sweater. The static electricity will hold the balloon to the sweater.

Never touch an electrical socket. Electricity can kill you.

▷ To light the bulb, electricity flows from the battery, down the wire, through the bulb, and back to the battery. This is called a circuit.

battery

wire

bulb

◁ Electricity is important in our daily lives. None of these machines could work without it. They all use electricity.

Find out more

Cars
Energy
Light
Trains
Weather

Energy

Light, sound, and heat are all forms of energy. Energy can move from place to place, but it is usually carried by something. Sound is carried by the air, and electricity is carried by wires. Energy to light and heat our homes is made by burning coal, oil, or gas, but some can be made by wind and water. Some forms of energy can make things move. You use energy when you run or jump.

△ You can use your energy to make things happen. This girl is using her energy to blow. This makes the vanes of the pinwheel spin around.

▷ The Sun provides the energy for trees and plants.

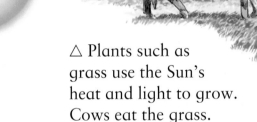

△ Plants such as grass use the Sun's heat and light to grow. Cows eat the grass.

△ Cows use the energy from the grass to make milk.

◁ This energy helps us walk, run, jump, and talk.

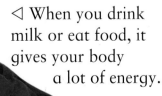

◁ When you drink milk or eat food, it gives your body a lot of energy.

stored
energy

movement
energy

△ Energy never
disappears, but it can
be stored. When you push back on
a swing, you are storing some energy.

△ When you let go,
the energy changes
from stored energy to movement
energy, and you move forward.

oil

coal

gas

◁ The Sun's
energy is stored
in oil, coal, and
gas. These were
made millions of
years ago from
dead plants. We
burn them to
make electricity.

△ Gasoline is made from oil. The gas is
burned by the car's engine. This releases
energy and makes the car move.

▷ Burning gas and diesel fuel can cause pollution. This is mainly caused by the exhaust fumes from cars, trucks, buses, and motorcycles.

▽ This car uses solar power to run. The panels collect light from the Sun. The light makes energy to turn the wheels.

solar-powered car

△ Energy made from water is called hydroelectric power. The water is stored behind a dam. As it flows down a pipe, it creates electricity by driving a generator.

◁ Windmills on a wind farm can also make electricity. Solar power, water, and wind energy do not cause air pollution.

Find out more

Cars
Earth
Electricity
Food
Health
Light
Sun

Europe

Europe is the second-smallest continent —only Australia is smaller. It stretches from the snowy Arctic in the north to the warm lands of the Mediterranean Sea in the south. It has high mountains, large forests, and many rivers. Many people live in Europe, and some parts are very crowded. Most people live in or near cities.

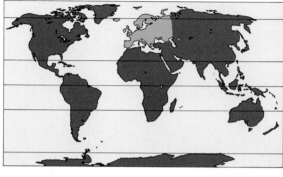

△ Europe is shown in green on this map. Europe has a ragged outline. In the east, it is joined to Asia.

◁ The peacock butterfly is found in gardens, woods, and mountains all over Europe, except in the cold north.

peacock butterfly

▽ St. Basil's Cathedral is in Moscow, the capital city of Russia. Russia is the largest country in the world. It stretches across Europe and Asia.

△ This is a beach in Amalfi, Italy, in southern Europe. Millions of tourists spend their vacations in the warm countries around the Mediterranean Sea.

◁ In Sweden, people dance around a Maypole on Midsummer's Eve to mark the longest day of the year.

▽ Along the coast of Norway, in northern Europe, there are deep inlets of sea with steep sides called fjords.

▷ Olive trees grow in rows on the hot, dry hills of southern Spain. Many European countries grow olives and many other fruits.

◁ Budapest is the capital of Hungary. It used to be two cities— Buda and Pest. The Danube River ran between them. Now it flows through the middle of Budapest. There are many fine old buildings along the Danube's banks.

Find out more
History
Maps
World

Farming

All over the world, farmers grow crops and raise animals for food. They plant fields of wheat, rice, corn, oats, and vegetables. They raise animals for their meat, milk, and eggs. Many farms use machines to do most of the work. Some farms do all of the work by hand.

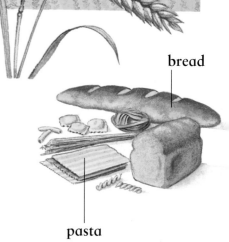

bread

pasta

▽ Rice is an important crop in China, India, and other countries in Asia. It is grown in flooded fields called paddies. It is usually sown and picked by hand.

▷ Wheat is almost always grown in huge fields. It is harvested by a combine. Wheat is ground into flour to make bread and pasta.

rice

△ Milk from cows is used to make dairy products such as cheese, butter, and cream.

△ Female chickens are called hens. They lay eggs. People eat meat and eggs from chickens.

◁ Large flocks of sheep are raised on sheep stations in Australia. Their wool is clipped off, cleaned, and spun into yarn.

◁ Pests, such as the Colorado potato beetle, destroy crops. Farmers spray crops with chemicals to kill the pests.

△ This tractor is spreading manure over a plowed field. Manure is a fertilizer. It feeds the soil and helps new crops grow large and strong.

Find out more

Asia

Australia and the Pacific Islands

Conservation

Europe

Colorado potato beetle

Fish

Fish live in water. Some live in the cold ocean, while others live in warm, shallow water. Fish are all different shapes and sizes. The huge but toothless whale shark can be up to 50 feet (15m) long. A tiny fish called a pygmy goby is no longer than your fingernail.

eye

fin

gill cover

fin

scale

tail

great white shark

◁ Great white sharks are fast swimmers and fierce hunters. They use their razor-sharp teeth to tear apart their prey.

▽ Blue marlins and many other big fish live far away from the shore. Tuna and mackerel live close to the surface of the ocean. Sawfish and rays live on the ocean floor.

blue marlin

tuna

mackerel

ray

sawfish

puffer fish

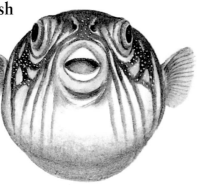

▷ A puffer fish can blow up its body like a balloon. It does this to scare away its enemies.

African cichlid

▷ The babies of the African cichlid fish swim into their mother's mouth to escape from danger.

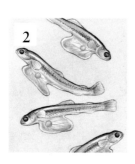

△ **1** A female salmon lays her eggs in the river where she was born. **2** When the eggs hatch, the babies are called fry.

△ **3** The young salmon live in the river for two years. **4** Then they swim down to the ocean. They return to the river to lay their eggs.

Fact box

• A fish is a vertebrate, which means that it has a backbone.

• Fish breathe by taking in oxygen from the water through their gills.

• Most fish swim through the water by moving their tails from side to side.

lionfish

▽ Fish that live in the warm, shallow water around coral reefs are often brightly colored. Their bold patterns act as camouflage and help them hide among the corals and creep up on their prey.

angelfish

parrot fish

butterfly fish

cowfish

Find out more

Animals
Fishing
Food
Oceans and seas
Prehistoric life
Water

Fishing

Rivers, seas, and oceans are full of fish and other creatures that people like to eat. Every day people set out in their fishing boats to catch different types of fish. They often use trawler boats. These have huge nets that can scoop up thousands of fish at a time.

◁ A large net bag is dragged behind a trawler. It can catch fish on the ocean floor.

trawler net

▷ Some fishing boats use special equipment called sonar to find schools of fish.

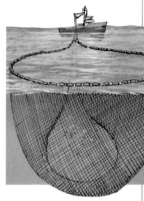

▷ A purse seine net is towed around a school of fish. The net is pulled up by a huge rope.

purse seine net

▷ Long drift nets are used to trap fish that swim near the surface of the water.

drift net

◁ A net full of fish is pulled onto a trawler. The fish are sorted and cleaned. Then they are packed in ice to keep them fresh.

Find out more

Australia and the Pacific Islands

Fish

Oceans and seas

Ships and boats

Water

Flowers

hanging basket

Most plants have flowers. Flowers are important because they help make the seeds that grow into new plants. This happens when a grain called pollen travels from one flower to another. Large, sticky pollen grains are carried by insects when they fly from flower to flower drinking nectar. Small, light grains are carried by the wind.

petal

stigma

stamen

carpel

sepal

△ These are the parts of a flower. Pollen is carried from the stamen of one flower to the stigma of another. This is called pollination.

▷ Flowers make nectar, from which bees makes honey. As a bee drinks the nectar, pollen sticks to its body. When it flies to another flower, some pollen rubs off onto that flower and pollinates it.

pollen

female catkins

pollen

male catkins

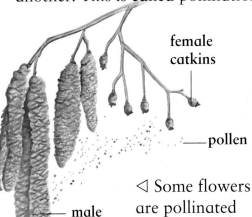

◁ Some flowers are pollinated by the wind. Pollen is blown from the male catkins to the female catkins.

 1    2   3    4

△ 1 The flowers of a pear tree are pollinated by insects. 2 Tiny fruits grow underneath the flowers. Inside each fruit are seeds.

△ 3 The fruits swell and grow. 4 When the fruits are ripe, animals break them open and the seeds are spread out.

Find out more

Conservation

Insects

Plants

Seasons

Water

Flying machines

There are all types of different flying machines, from hot-air balloons and gliders to helicopters and passenger planes. The fastest way to travel is by airplane. An airplane has wings to lift it up into the air and an engine to push it forward. For hundreds of years, people dreamed of being able to fly, but they were not successful until the early 1900s.

△ The first airplane was built by the Wright brothers in the early 1900s. The pilot had to lie on his stomach in order to fly it.

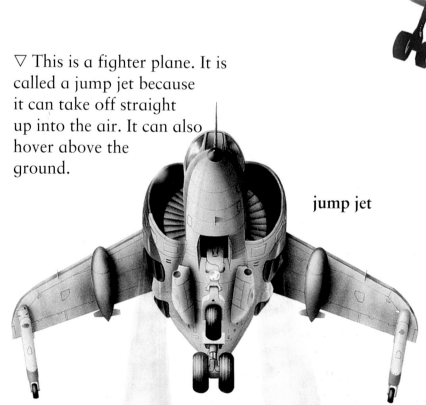

▷ This passenger jet can carry around 250 people. Jumbo jets are the largest passenger planes in the world. They can carry more than 800 people.

▽ This is a fighter plane. It is called a jump jet because it can take off straight up into the air. It can also hover above the ground.

jump jet

hot-air balloon

△ The air inside a hot-air balloon is heated by a powerful gas burner. Because hot air rises, it makes the balloon float up into the sky.

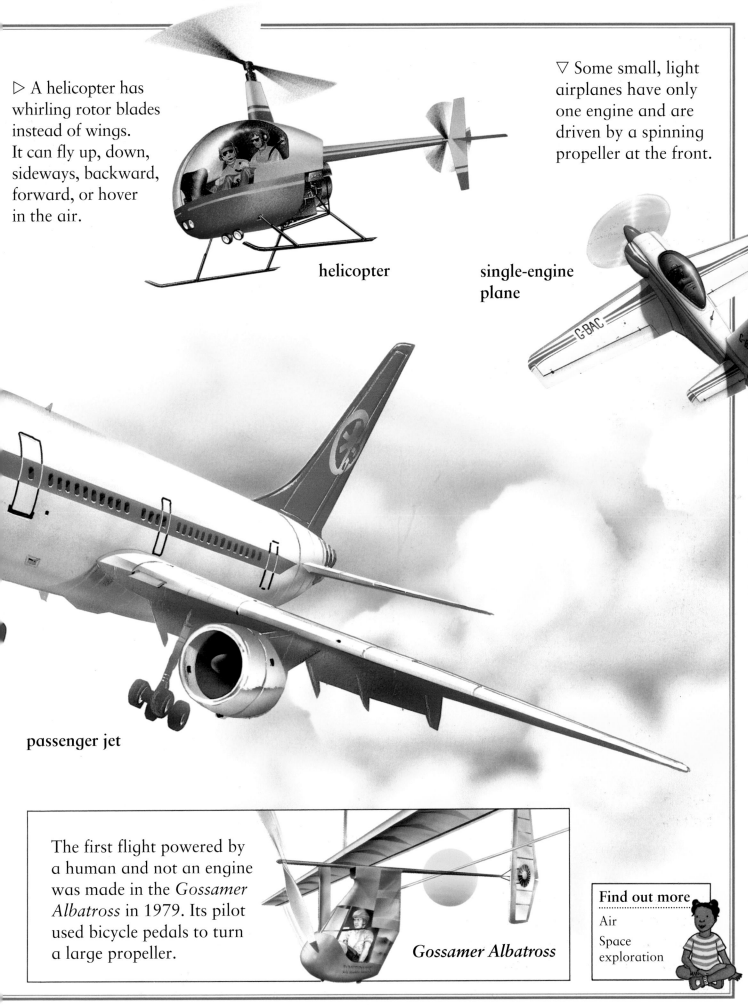

▷ A helicopter has whirling rotor blades instead of wings. It can fly up, down, sideways, backward, forward, or hover in the air.

helicopter

▽ Some small, light airplanes have only one engine and are driven by a spinning propeller at the front.

single-engine plane

passenger jet

The first flight powered by a human and not an engine was made in the *Gossamer Albatross* in 1979. Its pilot used bicycle pedals to turn a large propeller.

Gossamer Albatross

Find out more
Air
Space
exploration

Food

Everybody needs food. It gives you energy to move and stay warm. It helps you grow and get better when you are sick. To stay healthy, you need proteins, fats, carbohydrates, fiber, and vitamins, as well as water to drink. Eating too much sugary or fatty food is unhealthy.

proteins

△ Milk, meat, eggs, nuts, and fish give you proteins that build your body and help it stay strong.

▷ Fruits and vegetables have fiber. Fiber helps the food you eat pass through your body.

fiber

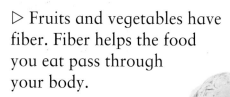

fats

△ Fats from foods such as butter, milk, cheese, bacon, and oil give you energy, but it is best not to eat large amounts of fat.

carbohydrates

△ Carbohydrates give your body a lot of energy. Foods such as bread, pasta, potatoes, beans, and rice all have carbohydrates in them.

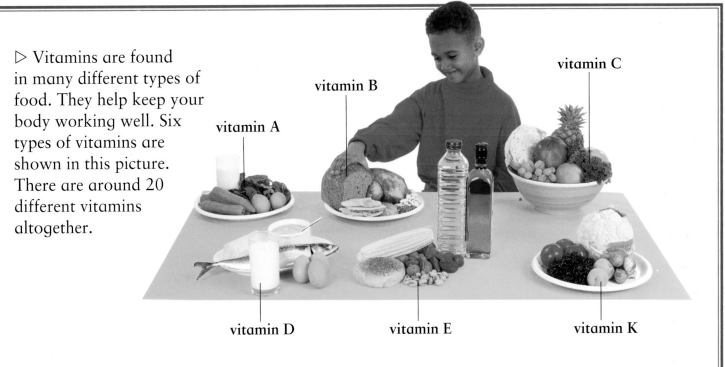

▷ Vitamins are found in many different types of food. They help keep your body working well. Six types of vitamins are shown in this picture. There are around 20 different vitamins altogether.

vitamin A

vitamin B

vitamin C

vitamin D

vitamin E

vitamin K

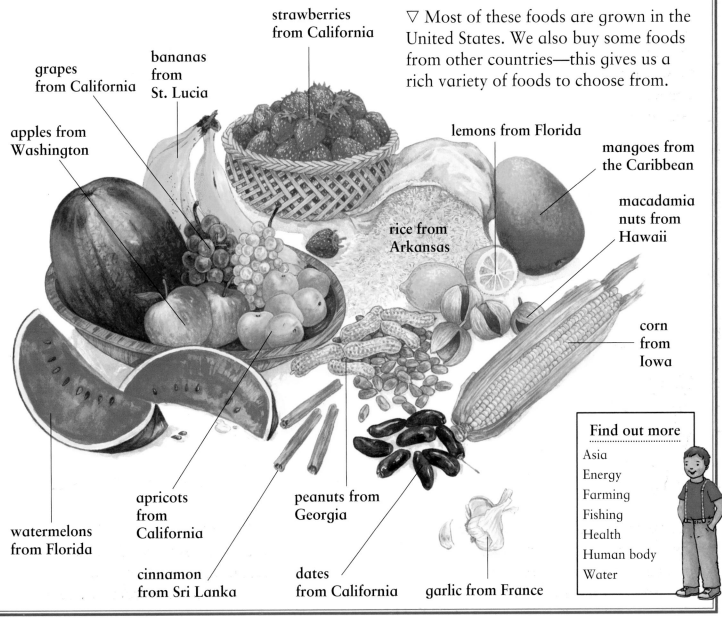

strawberries from California

▽ Most of these foods are grown in the United States. We also buy some foods from other countries—this gives us a rich variety of foods to choose from.

grapes from California

bananas from St. Lucia

apples from Washington

lemons from Florida

mangoes from the Caribbean

macadamia nuts from Hawaii

rice from Arkansas

corn from Iowa

watermelons from Florida

apricots from California

cinnamon from Sri Lanka

peanuts from Georgia

dates from California

garlic from France

Find out more

Asia
Energy
Farming
Fishing
Health
Human body
Water

Forests

The forests that grow in cold, dry parts of Earth have very different types of trees from the forests that grow in warm, wet parts of the world.

A forest is home to many animals. The trees give them food and shelter them from the sun, rain, and wind.

△ Look at all of these things. Wood from trees has been used to make them. Even the pages of this book are made from wood.

◁ Rainforests grow in hot, wet places. More than half of the world's animals and plants live in these forests. Huge areas of rainforests are cut down each year. This means that many of the animals and plants there could die out.

deciduous forest

◁ Deciduous forests are full of trees that lose their leaves in the fall. New leaves grow in the spring.

white-tailed deer

jay

badger

△ The badger lives in an underground home called a set. It hunts in the forest at night.

△ A deer's spots make it hard to see in the forest. This is called camouflage.

◁ Jays eat the acorns from oak trees. They often bury the acorns and then dig them up in the winter, when it is hard to find food.

coniferous forest

▷ Forests in cold places are full of coniferous trees. They keep their leaves all through the year.

moose

chipmunk

◁ A moose is a very large deer. It feeds on water plants and young tree shoots.

△ A chipmunk uses pouches in its cheeks to carry nuts and seeds back to store in its burrow.

Find out more
Buildings
Conservation
Mountains
Trees
Trucks

Fossils

Fossils are what is left of plants and animals long after they die. Scientists study fossils to find out about life on Earth millions of years ago. When the plants and animals died, what was left of them very slowly turned to stone.

▷ More than 200 years ago 12-year-old Mary Anning found a huge fossil on a cliff. It was a reptile called *Plesiosaurus* that lived in the sea millions of years ago.

△ 1 Ammonites lived in the sea millions of years ago. 2 When one died, its soft body rotted away. Layers of mud buried its hard shell.

△ 3 Over thousands of years, the mud hardened and turned to rock, and the shell became a fossil. 4 Many years later, the fossil was dug up.

spider in amber

△ This spider has been kept whole in amber. Amber is sticky tree sap that has dried and hardened.

▷ This woolly mammoth was frozen for thousands of years in the icy ground of Siberia in Russia.

woolly mammoth

◁ Fossils of plants are often found in large lumps of coal. This is a type of fern.

Find out more

Dinosaurs
Prehistoric life

Grasslands

Grasslands cover huge areas of the world. These lands are sometimes too dry for many trees to grow there. Grasses are tough plants that grow quickly.

The hot grassland of Africa is called the savanna, and in Australia it is called the bush. Grasslands are called pampas in South America, prairies in North America, and steppes in Asia.

▽ The African savanna often looks brown and dry. In the short rainy season, it is fresh and green.

△ In Australia, the bush may catch on fire in the dry season. The ashes that are left become part of the soil.

△ Huge areas of the prairies of North America are used to grow wheat.

◁ This type of grass grows on the pampas of South America. It has long, feathery flowers.

pampas grass

Find out more
Africa
Asia
Camouflage
Farming
North America
South America

Health

You need to be healthy to keep your body working properly. A healthy diet gives your body energy and helps it grow and repair itself. Exercise helps your body grow and stay strong. Caring for yourself will keep you strong and healthy. Staying clean helps kill the germs that can cause sickness.

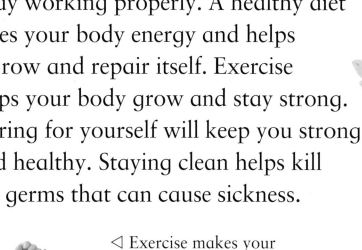

△ To get all of the things you need for a strong, healthy body, you have to eat many different foods. You also have to drink a lot of water.

◁ Exercise makes your muscles strong and keeps your body healthy. Playing soccer and other active games is a good way to exercise.

▽ Washing with soap and water keeps your skin clean. Staying clean stops germs from spreading.

Fact box

• The outside of your teeth is protected with hard enamel. Sugary foods and drinks eat the enamel away.

• People are given injections called vaccinations to keep them from getting sick.

• Most children sleep for around ten hours every night.

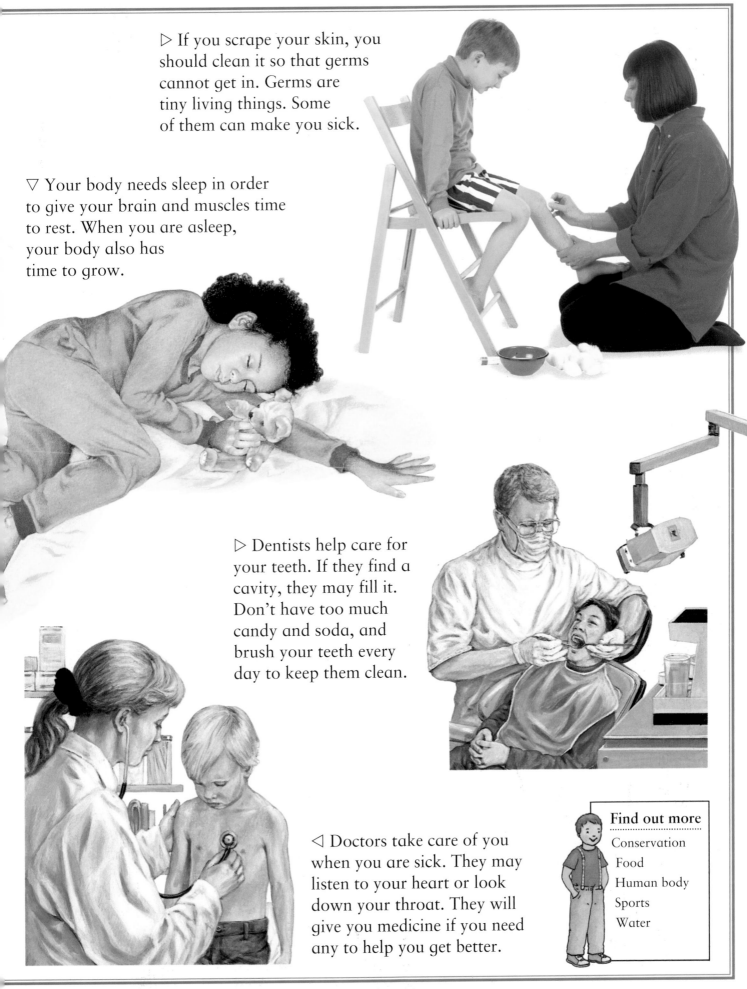

▷ If you scrape your skin, you should clean it so that germs cannot get in. Germs are tiny living things. Some of them can make you sick.

▽ Your body needs sleep in order to give your brain and muscles time to rest. When you are asleep, your body also has time to grow.

▷ Dentists help care for your teeth. If they find a cavity, they may fill it. Don't have too much candy and soda, and brush your teeth every day to keep them clean.

◁ Doctors take care of you when you are sick. They may listen to your heart or look down your throat. They will give you medicine if you need any to help you get better.

Find out more

Conservation
Food
Human body
Sports
Water

History

History is the study of what happened in the past. Historians discover facts about the past by reading old books and documents. They find clues in paintings, old buildings, maps, and photographs. Archaeologists study the past by looking for things people made and used. They search for ruined buildings and buried objects, such as tools, weapons, and pots, which tell them how people lived long ago.

△ Older people can tell you about events and daily life when they were young. Their childhood was probably very different from yours.

◁ Archaeologists can find clues about the past in tombs, houses, and bones by digging underground.

▷ Reading books about history is a good way to find out about the past. Television and radio have history programs, too.

△ Museums display objects from all over the world. Seeing these objects can help all of us learn about how people lived in the past.

Ancient Egypt

Some Egyptian pharaohs were buried in pyramids. Their bodies were rowed down the Nile River and sealed inside these large buildings.

△ Studying sites like the pyramids tells us that the Egyptians could carve hard stone and that they treated their dead rulers with great respect.

Ancient Greece

The Greeks performed plays in open-air theaters. They had a circular floor called an orchestra for dancing, with a stage behind. All the parts were played by male actors who wore masks.

△ There are ruins of many Greek theaters that tell us how the theaters would have looked.

Ancient China

The Great Wall of China is the longest wall ever built. It was built to keep out enemy tribes. The wall had towers for guards to keep watch.

▷ Some of the Great Wall of China still stands today. People can walk along the top.

Ancient Americas

The Aztecs ruled a mighty empire in what is now Mexico. They were fierce warriors. They built pyramids with temples on top, where they made offerings to their gods.

△ Aztec men fastened their cloaks with brooches. This is one made of gold and turquoise.

World War II
Many cities, such as Cologne in Germany, were bombed during World War II. The war lasted from 1939 to 1945, and millions of people died in it.

▷ After the war, new buildings were built in Cologne to replace those that had been destroyed. This photograph shows how the city looks today.

◁ No one knows who carved these enormous stone heads on Easter Island in the Pacific Ocean. We are still learning about the past, but some things may always be a mystery.

Find out more
Art and artists
Books
Castles
Kings

Human body

Every person is an individual. That means that no two people are exactly alike. Although you may look and sound different from everyone else, your body has all the same parts as theirs. Each of these parts has an important job to do. They are what make you human. They help you stand up, think, and be strong and healthy. They help you work and play.

△ The shape of our eyes, ears, noses, and mouths, as well as the color of our hair and skin, make us look different from one another.

The five senses
You can hear, see, smell, taste, and feel things. These are called your five senses. Messages go from your ears, eyes, nose, mouth, and skin to your brain. These tell you what the world is like and what is happening to your body.

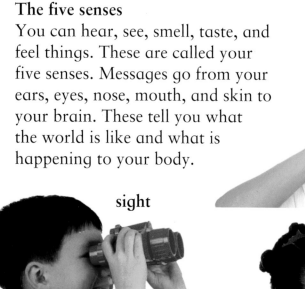

hearing

taste

sight

touch

smell

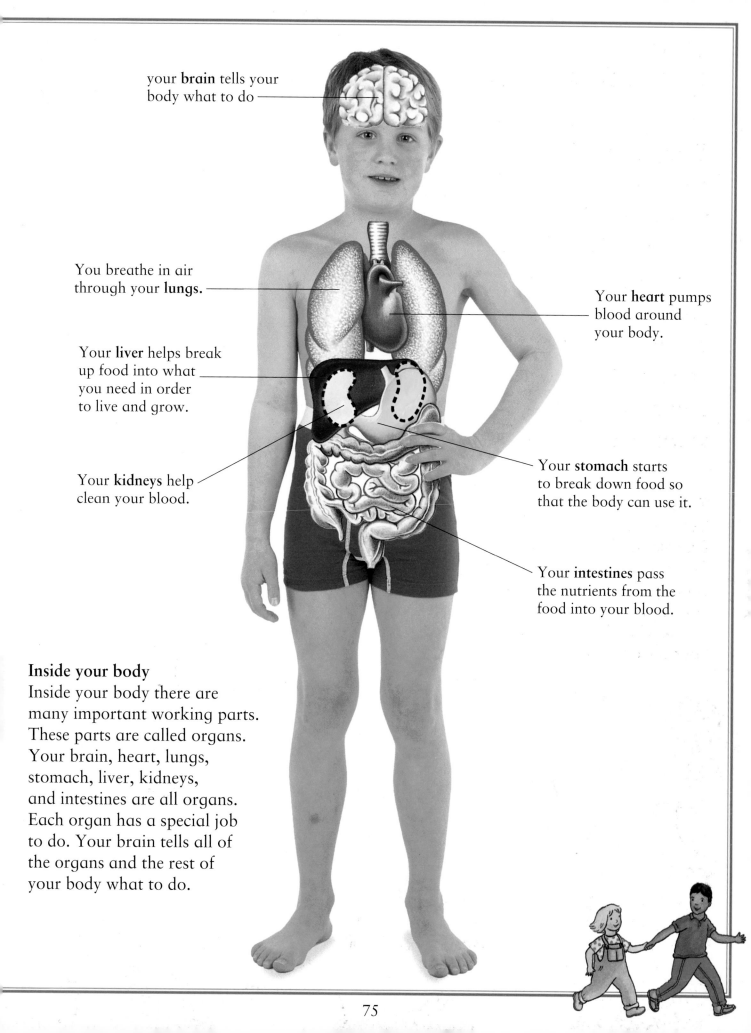

your **brain** tells your
body what to do

You breathe in air
through your **lungs.**

Your **liver** helps break
up food into what
you need in order
to live and grow.

Your **kidneys** help
clean your blood.

Your **heart** pumps
blood around
your body.

Your **stomach** starts
to break down food so
that the body can use it.

Your **intestines** pass
the nutrients from the
food into your blood.

Inside your body
Inside your body there are
many important working parts.
These parts are called organs.
Your brain, heart, lungs,
stomach, liver, kidneys,
and intestines are all organs.
Each organ has a special job
to do. Your brain tells all of
the organs and the rest of
your body what to do.

75

Skeleton

You have more than 200 bones in your body. They are joined together to make your skeleton. Bones are hard and strong. They support your body and get bigger as you grow.

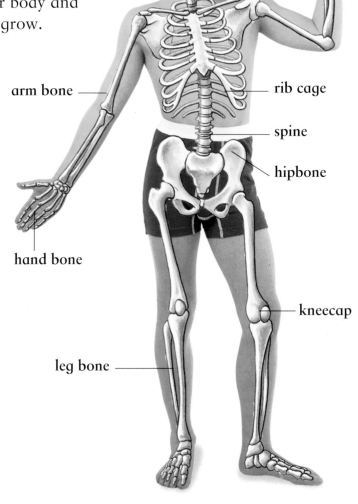

skull

arm bone

rib cage

spine

hipbone

hand bone

kneecap

leg bone

Muscles

All over your body you have muscles. These pull on your bones and make your body move. Muscles are joined to your bones by tough strips called tendons. Muscles grow stronger with exercise.

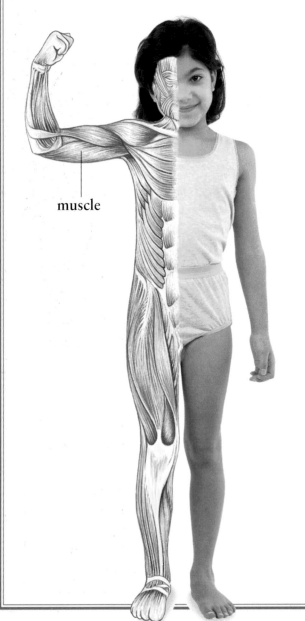

muscle

Breathing in

You breathe fresh air into your lungs. They fill up. Inside your lungs oxygen is taken from the air and passed into your blood where it is needed.

air in

windpipe

lung

Circulation

Your heart is a big muscle. As it beats, it pumps blood around your body. Blood carries the food and oxygen that your body needs to every part of the body. Blood flows through your body in tubes called arteries and veins.

heart

artery

vein

Skin

Tough, stretchy skin covers your whole body, and it has several layers. Skin protects all the parts inside you and keeps out dirt and germs. Your hair grows from roots in the skin, and you sweat through your skin.

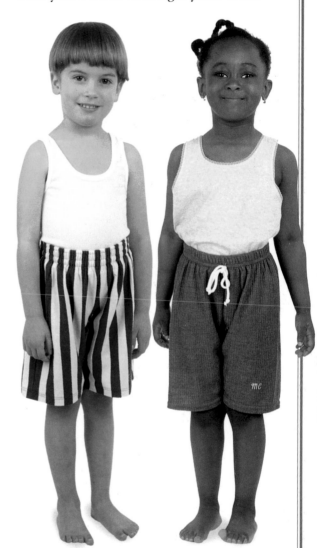

Breathing out

When you breathe out, your lungs empty, and the air in them is forced out. The used air contains carbon dioxide. This has been cleaned from the blood.

ir out

windpipe

lung

Find out more
Babies
Energy
Food
Health
Mammals
X-rays

Insects

Insects are animals with six legs. Most insects are tiny and have wings. Even the largest insect, the goliath beetle, is only 4 inches (10cm) long. Many insects are brightly colored, and some look like leaves or twigs to help them hide from their enemies.

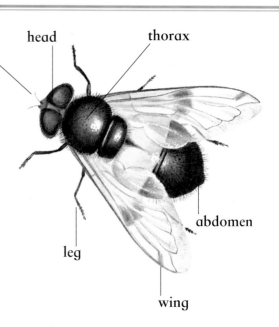

antenna
head
thorax
abdomen
leg
wing

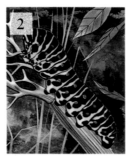

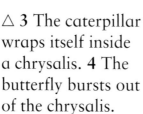

adult swallowtail butterfly

△ 1 A female butterfly lays eggs on a plant that her young will eat. A caterpillar hatches from each egg.
   2 The caterpillar eats greedily and grows quickly.

△ 3 The caterpillar wraps itself inside a chrysalis. 4 The butterfly bursts out of the chrysalis.

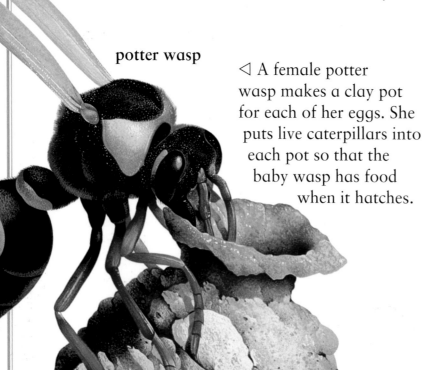

potter wasp

◁ A female potter wasp makes a clay pot for each of her eggs. She puts live caterpillars into each pot so that the baby wasp has food when it hatches.

△ The dragonfly is the fastest insect. It flies over ponds, streams, and rivers hunting other insects to eat.

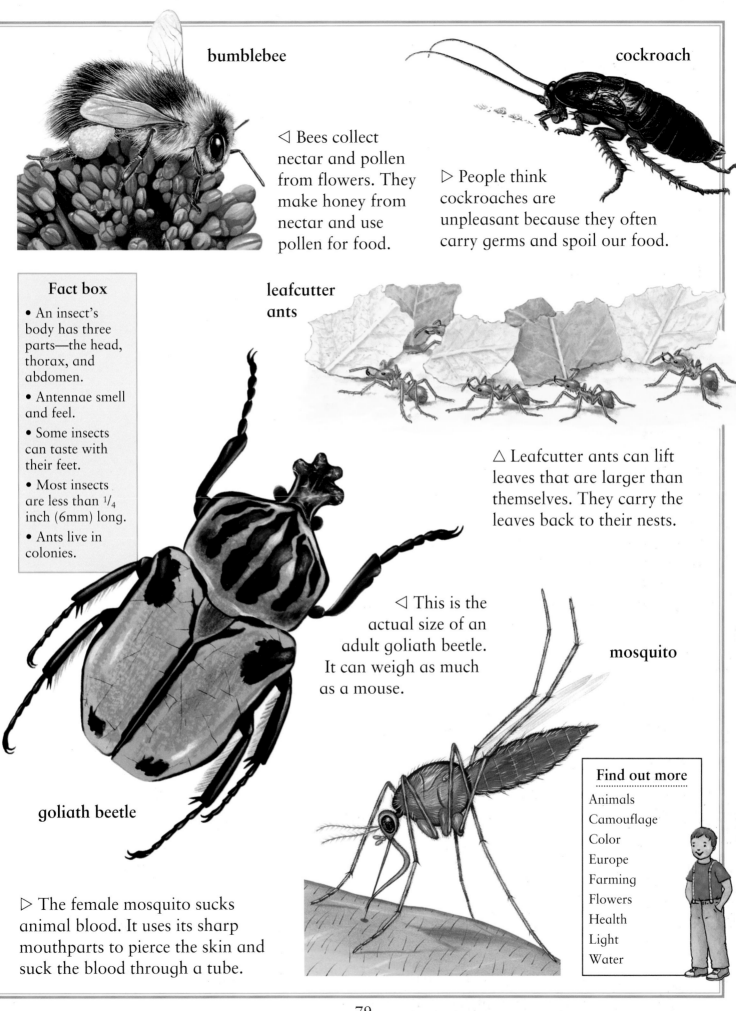

bumblebee

cockroach

◁ Bees collect nectar and pollen from flowers. They make honey from nectar and use pollen for food.

▷ People think cockroaches are unpleasant because they often carry germs and spoil our food.

leafcutter ants

Fact box

• An insect's body has three parts—the head, thorax, and abdomen.
• Antennae smell and feel.
• Some insects can taste with their feet.
• Most insects are less than $1/4$ inch (6mm) long.
• Ants live in colonies.

△ Leafcutter ants can lift leaves that are larger than themselves. They carry the leaves back to their nests.

◁ This is the actual size of an adult goliath beetle. It can weigh as much as a mouse.

mosquito

goliath beetle

Find out more
Animals
Camouflage
Color
Europe
Farming
Flowers
Health
Light
Water

▷ The female mosquito sucks animal blood. It uses its sharp mouthparts to pierce the skin and suck the blood through a tube.

Inventions

Inventions are things that have been discovered or created so that we can do something better. Some inventions make it possible to do things we have not been able to do before. Many make life more comfortable or improve our health. Others have changed the way we travel or have given us new ways to speak to one another.

△ Long ago, people discovered it was easier to roll heavy things. So they invented the wheel.

wheel

refrigerator

△ A refrigerator keeps foods and drinks cool. Food stays fresher for longer. Before refrigerators were invented, people kept food cool with large blocks of ice.

▽ Plastic is made in factories by using chemicals. It is a useful invention because it is easy to shape and it is tough. Many things are plastic.

▷ Television brings pictures and sounds from all over the world into our homes. In the United States, people watch around 50 hours of TV per week.

television

▽ An incubator is a warm, closed bassinet. It protects sick babies and babies who are born early. They stay there until they are strong and healthy.

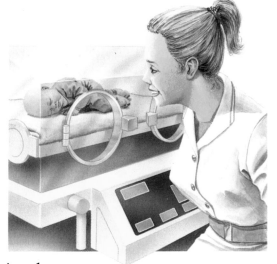

▷ This is a very old telescope. It was built by Galileo, a famous astronomer. An astronomer studies the stars and planets.

incubator

▽ Using a camera to take photographs is an easy way to keep a record of people, places, and events you have seen.

▽ The invention of the telephone makes it possible for you to talk to someone else almost anywhere in the world.

telescope

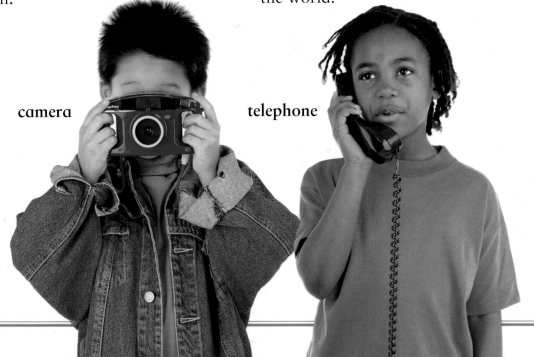

camera

telephone

Find out more

Bikes
Books
Cars
Computers
Flying machines
Trains
Space exploration

Jobs

People do all types of jobs. They may farm or fish. They may make things that others will sell. They may build homes, drive trucks, or care for sick people. People work mainly to earn money and may have several jobs during their lifetime.

△ Teachers work in schools. They help children learn the things they need to know.

△ Farming is an important job all over the world. This man is cutting sugar cane.

△ Many people work in offices. They use computers to help them.

△ Supermarkets provide jobs. This man is arranging food on the shelves.

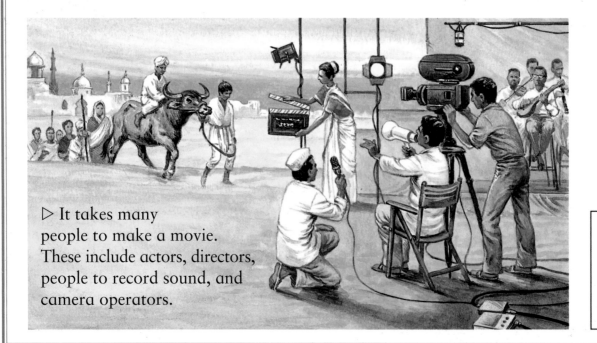

▷ It takes many people to make a movie. These include actors, directors, people to record sound, and camera operators.

Find out more
Books
Computers
Farming
Fishing

Kings

A king is a man who rules a country or people. Usually the king's son becomes the next king. Some kings are called chiefs or emperors. In the past, kings made laws and led their people into battle. Today, kings have less power. Most countries do not have kings.

△ This gold mask shows the face of Tutankhamen, an ancient Egyptian king. The Egyptian kings were called pharaohs.

▽ Kings once wore crowns as a sign of power. The British Crown Jewels are now worn only on special occasions.

△ This is the king of Tonga, a country in the Pacific Ocean, and his family at a wedding. His family has ruled Tonga for more than 200 years.

◁ Kings often lived in large houses called palaces or castles. This palace was the home of the emperors of China.

Find out more
Castles
History
Queens

Light

Almost all of our light comes from the Sun. Light is a type of energy. It travels from the Sun, through space, at a very high speed. Light is the fastest thing in the universe.

Light is made by things that are hot or burning. Flames, fireworks, and light bulbs all give off light. Some animals can make their own light.

△ During the day, we see by sunlight. At night, we use electric lights.

▷ Early peoples burned animal fat in stone lamps to make light. Later, candles were used. Two hundred years ago, people used oil lamps. Today we use electric lights.

wax candle

oil lamp

stone lamp

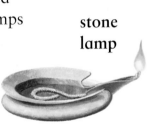

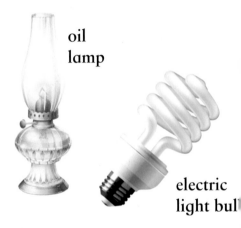

electric light bul

▽ A glowworm is a type of beetle that makes its own pale green light. The female uses the light to attract a mate in the dark.

glowworm

transparent

translucent

opaque

△ Glass is transparent. It lets all light pass through it. You can see through glass clearly.

△ Plastic is translucent. It lets some light through it. You can't see through plastic clearly.

△ Thick paper is opaque. It stops all light. You can't see through opaque things at all.

◁ Light always travels in straight lines. Light can spread out, but it cannot bend around things.

▷ Shadows are made when light hits things that it cannot shine through. The light is blocked so that a patch of darkness is made.

△ A reflection is made when light bounces off the surface of water into your eyes.

rainbow

△ A rainbow shows us the colors in sunlight. When the Sun shines through rain, the light is split up into all its different colors.

◁ A tomato looks red to you because it soaks up all the colors in sunlight— except red. The red bounces off of it, into your eyes.

Find out more

Antarctica and the Arctic

Color

Earth

Electricity

Plants

Sun

Machines

Machines are used to help people do things. Some machines are very complicated, with many moving parts. Others are very simple. We use simple machines every day. There are six types of simple machines: the lever, the wheel and axle, the slope, the wedge, the pulley, and the screw. All of these machines make it easier to move things.

△ Levers make it easier to lift things. This boy gently pushes down on the long handle to lift the lid off the can.

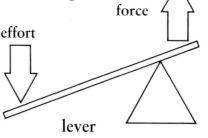

▽ The axle turns the wheels to move this tricycle along. It is much easier to roll a heavy object on wheels than it is to drag it across the ground.

wheel

axle

wheel and axle

▽ A slope makes it easier for this man to move the heavy wheelbarrow upward. It is easier to push it along instead of lifting it up.

force

effort

slope

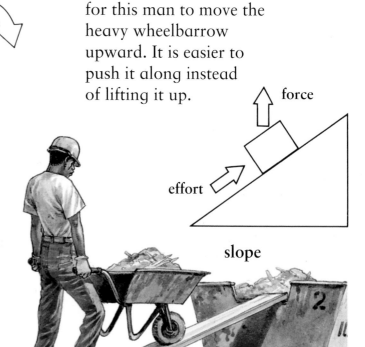

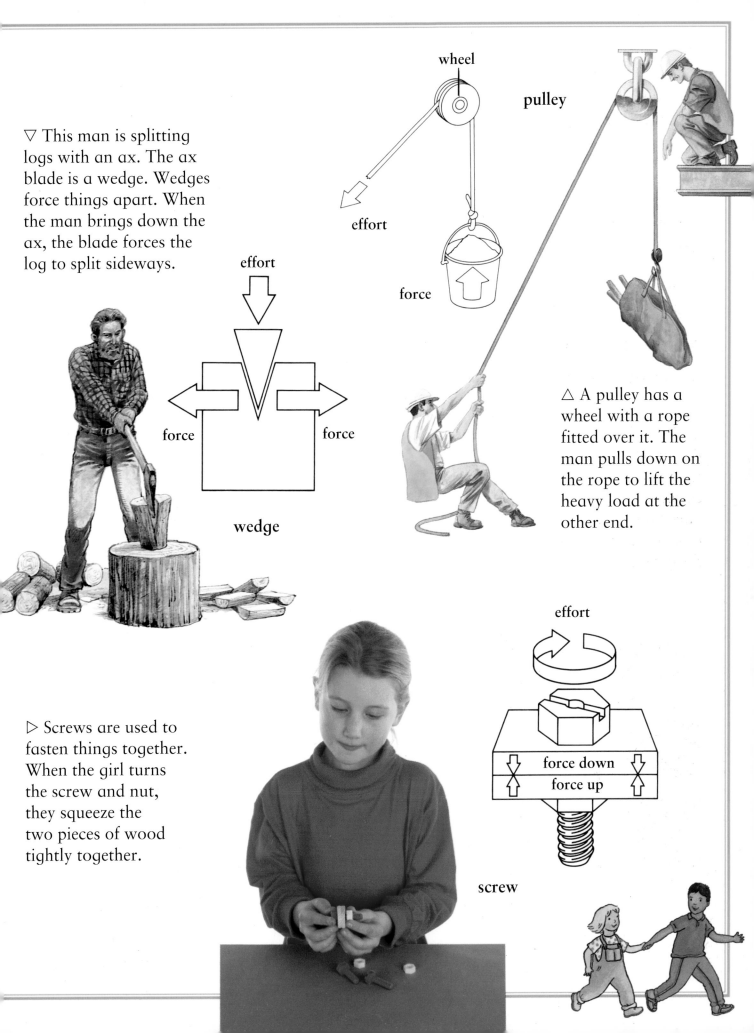

▽ This man is splitting logs with an ax. The ax blade is a wedge. Wedges force things apart. When the man brings down the ax, the blade forces the log to split sideways.

effort

force   force

wedge

wheel

pulley

effort

force

△ A pulley has a wheel with a rope fitted over it. The man pulls down on the rope to lift the heavy load at the other end.

effort

force down
force up

screw

▷ Screws are used to fasten things together. When the girl turns the screw and nut, they squeeze the two pieces of wood tightly together.

Complicated machines

Several simple machines can be put together to make much more complicated machines.

scale

lever

clock

cog

△ Clocks have cogs inside them. Cogs are wheels with teeth. As they turn, the teeth of one cog fit between those of another. The cogs in a clock turn the hour hand and the minute hand at different speeds.

△ This type of weighing scale is a lever. When a load is put in one bowl, it is heavier and it falls. The other bowl rises. If each bowl has an equal load, the scale balances and the bowls are level.

pulley wheel

△ The arm of this tower crane is a lever. Heavy weights on one end balance the load on the other end. Several pulley wheels make lifting easier.

tower crane

Find out more
Bikes
Books
Computers
Electricity
Farming
Flying machines
Trains

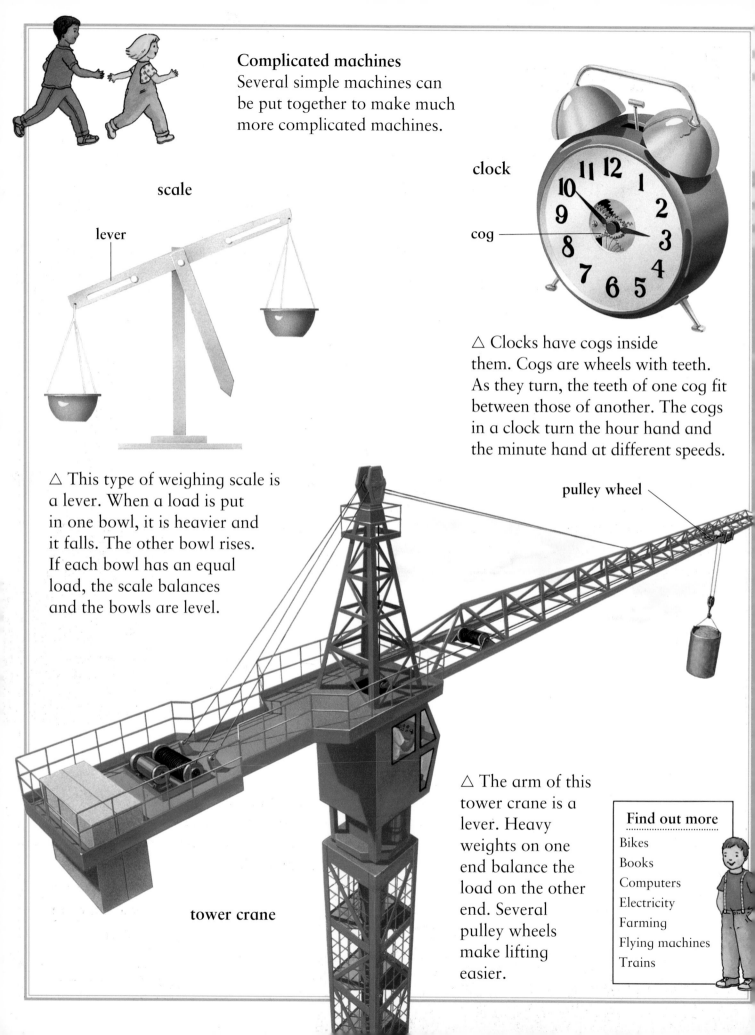

Magnets

Magnets attract, or pull, certain things toward them. Objects made of some metals, such as iron and steel, are attracted to a magnet. Materials that are attracted to a magnet are called magnetic. Most materials, such as wood, cloth, paper, glass, and plastic, and most metals are not magnetic.

▷ The end of each magnet is called a pole. The south pole of one magnet attracts the north pole of another.

▷ You can find out for yourself which things are magnetic. Collect a pile of objects and see how many you can pick up with a magnet. Can you spot the magnetic things in this picture?

◁ Giant magnets like this one are used to pick up and move huge pieces of metal such as old cars.

Find out more
....
Metals

Mammals

Mammals are vertebrate animals. They are warm-blooded and have body hair. Most give birth to live babies, not eggs that hatch later. Young mammals can drink their mother's milk.

The biggest mammal is the blue whale. It is around 100 feet (31m) long and weighs more than 100 tons.

rabbit

△ A rabbit gives birth to many babies at the same time. A mother rabbit cares for her young until they can take care of themselves.

◁ Humans are mammals, too. We give birth to live babies. Humans depend on their parents for a long time.

humans

▷ A kangaroo is a marsupial, which is a mammal that carries its young in a pouch. A baby kangaroo is called a joey.

kangaroo

joey

▷ Lions live in family groups called prides. They are good hunters and eat meat. A lioness cares for her cubs and teaches them how to hunt.

lion

cubs

mole

▽ A mole is a burrowing mammal. It has strong front legs and big claws. These are used for digging holes called burrows.

dolphins

bat

◁ Dolphins are mammals that live all of their lives in the sea. Unlike fish, they have to come up to the surface to breathe air.

△ Bats are the only mammals that can fly. A bat has a furry body. Its wings are made of soft, smooth skin.

chimpanzees

Fact box

• Most mammals have either hair or fur.

• Mammals are warm-blooded. This means that the temperature of their bodies stays the same in both hot and cold weather.

• A mammal is a vertebrate. This means that it has a backbone.

• Mammals have larger brains than other animals.

▽ The duck-billed Australian platypus is an unusual mammal because it lays eggs and does not give birth to live young.

duck-billed platypus

△ Chimpanzees live in family groups. They often comb each other's hair with their fingers. They also pick off dirt and insects.

Etruscan shrew

lioness

△ The tiny Etruscan shrew weighs no more than a large sugar cube.

Find out more

Animals

Australia and the Pacific Islands

Babies

Caves

Grasslands

Human body

Prehistoric life

Soil

Maps

A map is a carefully drawn picture that shows you what a place looks like from high up above it. Maps show where roads and rivers are. They can help you find your way from one place to another. Maps show a large area of land as much smaller than it really is. A book of maps is called an atlas.

▽ Make a map of the area around your home. Draw in the streets and add any important landmarks such as your school and church, the local park, and any stores.

△ From the air, the area around the Eiffel Tower in Paris looks like this.

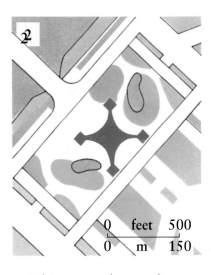

```
0      feet    500
0       m     150
```

△ This map shows the small area around the Eiffel Tower in detail.

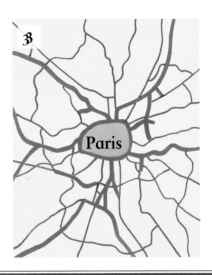

◁ The road map on the left shows a much larger area. You can see Paris but not the Eiffel Tower.

◁ This map shows all of France. You can see Paris, but you can't see all of the roads around the city.

Find out more

World

Measuring

If you want to find out exactly how heavy or tall things are, you can measure them by using different instruments. In the past, people used their hands, arms, or feet for measuring. This was a problem because no one was the same size, so everyone agreed to use the same measurements—such as inches.

▽ Long ago, the Egyptians used hand spans, like this, to measure how long or wide things were. Today, we use rulers or tape measures and measure in inches and feet or centimeters and meters.

◁ Scales are used to find out how heavy people and things are. This is called weight. Weight is measured in pounds and ounces or kilograms and grams.

▷ You use a ruler or tape measure to find out how long or high something is. Length and height are measured in feet and inches or meters and centimeters.

▷ A measuring cup adds an exact amount of liquid. Liquids are measured in pints or liters.

Find out more

Antarctica and the Arctic

Time

Weather

Metals

Most metals are hard, shiny materials. They can be bent or hammered into different shapes. Iron, copper, and aluminum are three types of metals. Most metals come from ores, which are a mixture of metal and rock. The ore is dug out of the ground. Different metals can be mixed to make tough, new metals called alloys.

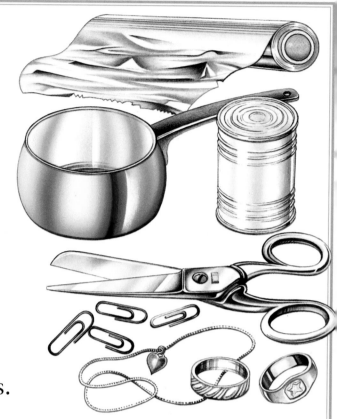

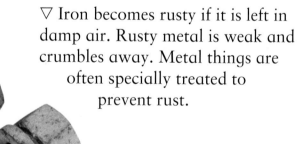

△ Aluminum is used to make foil, cans, and pipes; copper is used for pots and pans; steel for scissors and paper clips. Gold and silver are used to make jewelry.

▽ Iron becomes rusty if it is left in damp air. Rusty metal is weak and crumbles away. Metal things are often specially treated to prevent rust.

△ Iron ore is heated in a furnace. When it gets very hot, the iron melts. The iron is poured off, leaving the unwanted rock behind. The iron is then used to make steel.

Find out more

Buildings
Magnets
Money

Money

Money is used to pay for the things we want to buy. Coins and paper bills are money. Each coin and bill is worth a different amount. People use bills for large amounts. Bills are printed on special paper and with complicated patterns that are hard to fake, or copy.

△ Before money existed, people exchanged the things they needed. This is called bartering. The man on the left is bartering some cattle for armor.

▷ You can save your coins in a piggy bank. Put large amounts of money in a bank.

◁ Each country has its own type of money. For example, the United States uses dollars, Great Britain uses pounds, and France uses euros.

Find out more
Jobs
Metals

Moon

The Moon is our closest neighbor in space. It is a large ball of dusty rock with no air, water, wind, or weather. No animals or plants can live there. Daytime on the Moon is boiling hot, but at night it is very cold. The Moon looks bright in the sky because it reflects light from the Sun.

△ The Moon is covered with dents called craters. These were made when meteoroids crashed into the Moon. Meteoroids are large lumps of rock and metal.

▽ The Moon moves around Earth once every month. Its path is called an orbit.

full moon

△ There is a full moon once each month. The Sun shines on part of the Moon, and as the Moon orbits Earth, its shape seems to change.

▽ On July 20, 1969, two American astronauts were the first people to set foot on the Moon. They were Neil Armstrong and "Buzz" Aldrin.

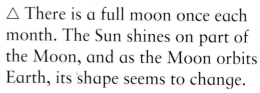

Find out more

Planets

Space exploration

Mountains

A mountain is a very high hill—an area that is much higher than the land around it. Mountains have steep sides. They are often much colder at the top. Some of the highest peaks are covered in snow all year long. Above a certain height called the timberline, the climate is too harsh for trees to grow.

◁ Skiing is a fast way to get across snow. It is a popular mountain sport.

mountain goat

trumpet gentian

△ Mountain goats have thick, woolly coats and are good climbers.

△ Mountain plants grow in low clumps. This is to protect them from the cold winds.

Find out more

Asia

Europe

Oceans and seas

South America

Volcanoes

Music

There are many different types of music, and most people like playing or listening to it. They may sing or play an instrument such as a piano or a guitar, by themselves or in a band or orchestra. People play music to celebrate special occasions, to entertain themselves or others, or just to relax. A person who plays an instrument is called a musician.

△ You probably listen to music on your MP3 player or CD player or hear it on the radio and television.

△ An orchestra is a large group of musicians who play a variety of different instruments. Orchestras often play music for concerts, operas, ballets, and plays.

▷ At celebrations in the Caribbean islands, steel bands play in the streets or on the beach. The steel drums are made out of specially shaped, empty oil drums.

▷ This Japanese robot can play the keyboard much faster than a human can. It can read music or play a tune that is stored in its memory.

WABOT - 2

▽ You can play music, too. You may already play the piano or the recorder. There are many other types of musical instruments. These children are creating music with their instruments.

triangle

cymbal

tambourine

◁ Wolfgang Amadeus Mozart was one of the world's most famous musicians. He played in public when he was a child, and he wrote his first piece of music when he was only five years old.

Find out more
Australia
Dance
Sound

North America

North America is the world's third-largest continent. In the north, it is cold and there are large forests and many lakes. In the south, there are hot deserts and thick rainforests. The middle is a huge area of flat grassland called the prairies. The Rocky Mountains are in the western part of the continent. Many North Americans live in busy, modern cities.

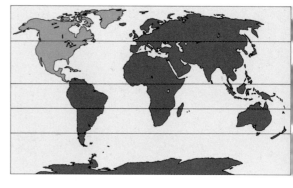

△ North America is shown in blue on this map. Most of it is covered by Canada, the United States, and Mexico.

◁ Many people visit Las Vegas, Nevada, a city built in the middle of the desert. At night, its brightly lit buildings shine against the dark sky.

△ People from other countries have come to live in North America. This picture shows some of the children and grandchildren of those people.

◁ A stall owner is getting ready for market day in Oaxaca (Wah-**ha**-ka) in Mexico. Mexican farmers were the first people to grow chilies, tomatoes, avocados, corn, and many types of beans.

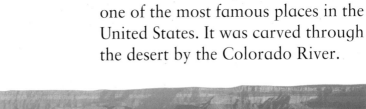

▽ The Grand Canyon in Arizona is one of the most famous places in the United States. It was carved through the desert by the Colorado River.

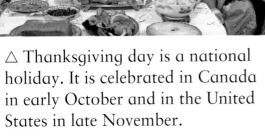

△ Thanksgiving day is a national holiday. It is celebrated in Canada in early October and in the United States in late November.

◁ Raccoons live in many parts of North America. They usually hunt at night for food.

raccoon

▷ Niagara Falls lies on the border between the United States and Canada. Tourists take boats to see the base of the falls.

◁ The Pueblos are Native Americans who live in the southwest. Long ago they lived in cliffs and were called "cliff dwellers."

Find out more

Buildings
Deserts
Grasslands
History
Sports
World
Years

Oceans and seas

There is more water than land on Earth's surface. You can travel around the world by boat without needing to touch land. There are four huge areas of water called oceans—the Pacific (the biggest and deepest ocean), the Atlantic, the Indian, and the Arctic. Seas are smaller areas of water.

△ Most waves are made by wind blowing across the water, and some are more than 30 feet (10m) high. Surfers ride on waves before they reach the shore.

◁ There are strange animals in the deepest, darkest parts of the ocean. Many have large mouths and glowing lights to help them catch their prey.

▽ At the bottom of the ocean there are flat areas, trenches, hills, and high mountains. Some islands are the tops of underwater volcanoes.

volcano

trench

ridge

▷ There are billions of tiny plants and animals floating in the sea. These are called plankton. Many fish and other ocean creatures feed on them.

plankton

sperm whale

◁ Whales are the largest creatures in the ocean. This sperm whale can grow up to 65 feet (20m) long.

▽ An octopus has eight long arms. If an octopus loses an arm, it grows a new one.

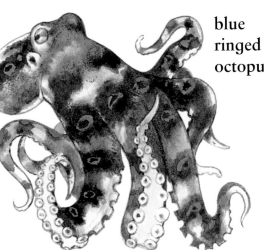

blue ringed octopus

▷ For hundreds of years, ships have sunk to the bottom of the sea. Divers sometimes find treasures in the remains of these ships.

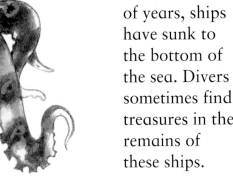

▽ Divers use small diving ships called submersibles to explore deep water. They go down to search for shipwrecks and to study ocean life.

submersible

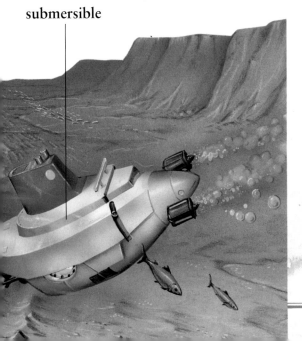

▽ Hot water bubbles up through holes like chimneys on the ocean floor. Blind crabs, giant worms, and other unusual creatures live near these rare hot spots.

worms

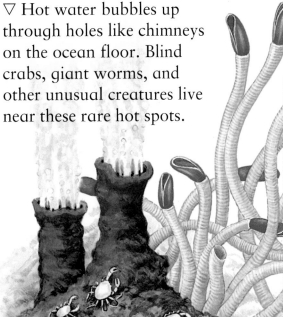

crabs

Find out more

Animals

Antarctica and the Arctic

Australia and the Pacific Islands

Fish

Fishing

Mammals

Seashores

Ships and boats

Water

World

Planets

Planets are huge balls of rock, metal, and gas that travel around a star. Earth is one of the eight planets that travel around our star, the Sun. The Sun and all of the planets, moons, and lumps of rock, dust, and ice that whirl around it make up our solar system. Earth has only one moon traveling around it, but some planets have several moons.

Sun

Earth

orbit

△ Planets travel around the Sun in paths called orbits. A complete orbit is called a year. For Earth, this is just over 365 days.

Fact box

- Mercury is the planet closest to the Sun.
- Venus is the hottest planet. It is covered with thick clouds of poisonous gas.
- Earth is the only planet with air and water.
- Mars is a red, rocky planet. It is very dry and has dust storms.

Jupiter

Earth

Mercury

Mars

Venus

Sun

Fact box

- Uranus orbits the Sun tilted on its side.

- Jupiter is the biggest planet. Its Great Red Spot is a giant hurricane that is about the same size as Earth.

- Saturn has the brightest rings of all the planets. It has at least 18 moons.

Pluto
(dwarf planet)

Uranus

Neptune

Fact box

- Saturn, Jupiter, Uranus, and Neptune are giant planets and are all made of gas and liquid.

- Freezing winds rip across Neptune's blue surface.

- Pluto used to be considered a planet. It is now classified as a dwarf planet.

Saturn

Find out more

Earth
Inventions
Moon
Space exploration
Sun
Universe

Plants

People and animals need plants for food. Plants also create oxygen, which is the invisible gas we need in order to live. When people breathe out, they release carbon dioxide gas into the air. Plants breathe this gas in, and it changes into other gases inside them. Plants breathe out the oxygen we need.

△ Most plants can make food from air, sunlight, and water. They take in water through their roots.

▽ Edelweiss grows in snowy places. It has hairs on its stalks and leaves that trap heat and protect it from the cold.

giant saguaro cactus

yellow iris

△ A giant saguaro cactus can be almost 60 feet (18m) tall and live for more than 200 years. These plants live in the hot, dry deserts of the southwest U.S. and Mexico. They store water in their thick stems.

edelweiss

white water lily   **yarrow**   **frogbit**   **water soldier**

◁ Some plants that grow in water have strong roots that hold them in the mud. Other plants just float in the water.

host plant   dodder

▷ Some plants cannot make their own food. The dodder plant is a parasite. This means that it attaches itself to another plant, called the host, and steals its food.

▷ Plants like ivy can "climb" up buildings or tall trees. Ivy holds onto rocks and walls using its tiny roots.

Boston ivy

shoot

1   2   3

▷ 1 A seed fills with water. It splits open and starts growing. 2 A root grows down into the soil. 3 A leafy shoot grows up out of the soil toward the sun.

bean seeds

root

▷ Daffodils and hyacinths grow from bulbs. The bulbs store food all through the winter. They grow into new plants in the spring.

bulb

fern

moss

△ Ferns and mosses do not have flowers or seeds. New plants grow from tiny bodies called spores.

▷ Mushrooms and toadstools are not plants. They are called fungi. Fungi have no roots, leaves, or stems. You can eat some mushrooms, but many fungi are poisonous.

Never touch, pick, or eat a toadstool.

Find out more
Conservation
Deserts
Farming
Flowers
Forests
Fossils
Grasslands
Mountains
Soil
Trees
Water

Prehistoric life

Earth is billions of years old. When it was first formed, there was no life at all. The first animals lived in the sea. Since then, millions of different types of animals have lived on Earth. Some have died out, but we know what they looked like by studying the fossils of their remains.

Earth was formed 4.6 billion years ago.

The first living things appeared in the sea 3.5 billion years ago.

Ichthyostega
(Ik-thee-o-stee-ga)

The first amphibians lived 370 million years ago.

△ *Ichthyostega* was one of the first amphibians. It lived on land and in the water.

All of the dinosaurs became extinct 65 million years ago.

▽ Dinosaurs died out 65 million years ago. Since life began on Earth, millions of types of animals have died out, and new ones have taken their place.

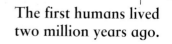

The first humans lived two million years ago.

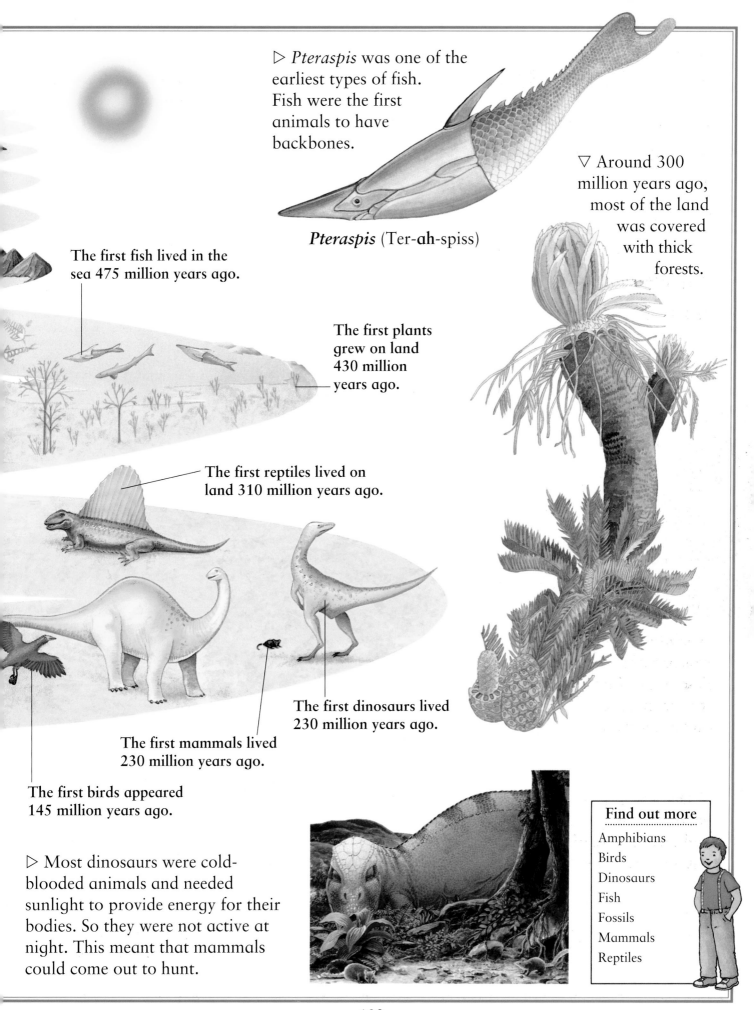

▷ *Pteraspis* was one of the earliest types of fish. Fish were the first animals to have backbones.

Pteraspis (Ter-**ah**-spiss)

▽ Around 300 million years ago, most of the land was covered with thick forests.

The first fish lived in the sea 475 million years ago.

The first plants grew on land 430 million years ago.

The first reptiles lived on land 310 million years ago.

The first dinosaurs lived 230 million years ago.

The first mammals lived 230 million years ago.

The first birds appeared 145 million years ago.

▷ Most dinosaurs were cold-blooded animals and needed sunlight to provide energy for their bodies. So they were not active at night. This meant that mammals could come out to hunt.

Find out more

Amphibians
Birds
Dinosaurs
Fish
Fossils
Mammals
Reptiles

Queens

A queen is a woman who rules a country or a kingdom. Sometimes the wife or mother of a king is called a queen. Queens can become rulers when their father, mother, or husband dies. Today there are only a few countries where a queen or a king rules.

△ The first stamp in the world was called the penny black. It had the head of the British Queen Victoria on it.

penny black

▷ Cleopatra was the last queen of ancient Egypt. She was very clever. She lost a war with the Romans. Some people say she let herself be bitten by a snake so that she died.

△ Queen Beatrix is the queen of the Netherlands. Like most rulers today, she visits many towns and cities to meet and talk to the people who live there.

◁ Elizabeth I was one of the most famous rulers of England. She was queen for 45 years and made England rich and powerful.

Find out more
Castles
History
Kings

Religion

There are many religions around the world, and the people who follow them have different beliefs and customs. Most religions have a god or gods and rules to help people live with one another. People who follow a religion may meet together in a special building. They usually have a special person, such as a priest, minister, or rabbi, to guide them. The most popular religions include Christianity, Islam, Judaism, Hinduism, Buddhism, and Sikhism.

church

△ Many people worship in special buildings. They may pray in a church, such as this one, or a mosque, temple, or synagogue.

Christians
These Christians are celebrating Easter Sunday. Christians believe that Jesus, the son of God, died on the cross and came back to life three days later. Easter celebrates his rising from the dead. His teachings are in the New Testament of the Bible.

Sikhs

Sikhs believe in one God and follow the teachings of gurus. They are taught to lead good, simple lives. The Golden Temple in Amritsar, India, is the most important holy place where Sikhs go to pray.

Hindus

Hindus worship many gods and believe the soul is reborn after death. Every year, Hindus celebrate Diwali, the festival of lights, to bring good fortune.

Jews

Here the candles are being lit during the eight-day festival of Hanukkah. Jews believe in one God, and their teachings and laws are written in the Torah.

Buddhists

Buddhists follow the teachings of an Indian prince who became known as Buddha. They say their prayers in front of statues of Buddha, such as this one.

Muslims

Followers of Islam are called Muslims. They believe in one God, called Allah, whose words were written down by the prophet Muhammad in the Koran. These Muslims are praying in the holy city of Mecca, the birthplace of Muhammad.

Other religions

There are many other religions, and each has its own festivals. Some religions worship the spirits of natural things such as trees and rocks. This is a fishing festival in Japan.

Find out more

Asia
Books
Dance
Europe
History
North America
South America

113

Reptiles

Lizards, crocodiles, turtles, and snakes are all reptiles. Reptiles have dry, scaly skin. Some reptiles live in water, and some live on land.

Most reptiles live in warm countries. Reptiles that live in cold places sleep through the winter and wake up in the spring. This is called hibernation.

△ Most snakes lay eggs with soft, leathery shells. The young snakes hatch when the eggs are warmed by the heat of the sun.

gecko

△ A gecko is a lizard with sticky pads on its toes. The pads allow it to run upside down on trees, rocks, and even ceilings.

◁ A crocodile mother cares for her young. When the babies hatch, their mother carries them carefully to the water in her huge mouth.

Nile crocodile

Fact box

• All reptiles are cold-blooded. This means that their body temperature is not constant. It changes as the temperature outside their bodies changes. They have to lie in the warm sun before they can move around. If they get too hot, they have to cool down in the shade.

▷ The frilled lizard spreads its collar and hisses loudly in order to frighten enemies away.

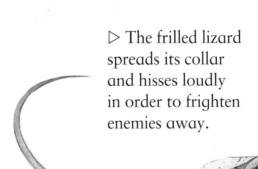

frilled lizard

green
turtle

◁ A turtle swims
using its strong
flippers. This turtle
lives in the sea,
but it lays its eggs
on the seashore.

▽ Many snakes have jaws
that stretch. They can open their
mouths very wide. Some snakes
can swallow a large animal whole.

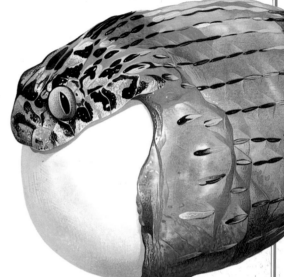

egg-eating snake

▷ The tortoise
lives on land. It
pulls its head and
legs into its shell
if it is scared.

tortoise

▽ The anaconda is a huge
snake from South America.
It coils its body around its
prey and squeezes it to death.

caiman

anaconda

▽ The Komodo dragon is the
largest lizard. It can grow up to
11.5 feet (3.5m) long. It attacks
deer and pigs.

Komodo
dragon

Find out more
Animals
Dinosaurs
Prehistoric life

Roads

Roads link one place to another. Cars, buses, and trucks travel on roads. There are special roads called highways or expressways, designed so that traffic can travel a long way without stopping. Signs and markings on roads tell drivers which way to go and how fast to travel.

△ Bridges and overpasses help traffic travel more quickly around crowded cities. Some roads go underground, through tunnels.

How a road is made
▷ Bulldozers shovel away trees and dirt.

bulldozer

scraper

◁ Scrapers make the ground level and smooth out a path. Scrapers are pulled by very large tractors.

dump truck

grader

◁ Dump trucks bring crushed rocks. Graders smooth this in place to make a flat base for the road.

roller

paving machine

△ A paving machine spreads on a mixture of stones, sand, and tar called asphalt. This is rolled flat.

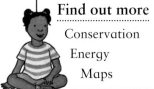

Find out more
Conservation
Energy
Maps

116

Science

Science is the study of the world around us. There are many types of sciences. Biology is the study of living things, geology is the study of Earth, and astronomy is the study of stars and planets. Scientists look at things and try to explain what they see. They set up experiments to test their ideas.

leaf under microscope

△ A microscope makes things look much larger. Scientists use all types of tools to help them understand the world around us.

sinks   floats

◁ You can be a scientist, too. These children are doing an experiment. First they guess which objects might float and which will sink. They sort them into piles.

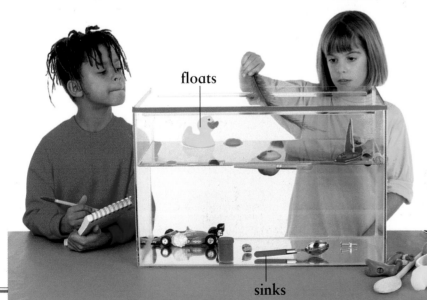

floats

sinks

◁ They drop the things from each pile into a tank of water to see if their guess was right. They think of reasons why some objects float and others sink. Do you know the reasons why?

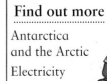

Find out more

Antarctica and the Arctic
Electricity

Seashores

The seashore is where the land meets the sea. Some seashores are sandy, and others may be rocky, muddy, or pebbly. Many different animals and plants live there. The seashore changes its shape all the time. This is because the waves pound against the beaches and rocks, slowly wearing them away.

▽ Many seabirds live on cliffs near the seaside. Puffins and gannets nest near the top, and murre lay their eggs on bare rocks.

puffin

gannet

murre

△ Twice each day the sea comes far up the shore. This is called high tide.

△ The sea also goes out again twice every day. This is called low tide.

◁ Sand is made up of very tiny pieces of broken rocks and shells. The color of sand depends on the color of the rocks it is made of.

Always use sunscreen and cover yourself to protect against the sun's harmful rays.

Find out more
Animals
Birds
Caves
Europe
Fossils
Oceans and seas

Seasons

Most of the world has four seasons. These are spring, summer, fall, and winter. This is because Earth is tilted. As Earth goes around the Sun, half of the world leans closer to the Sun. This means that half of Earth is warmer.

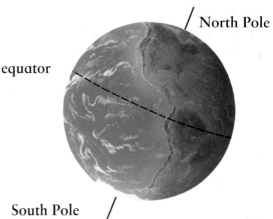

North Pole

equator

South Pole

△ It is the summer in the southern part of the world when it faces the Sun. In the northern part, it is the winter.

◁ Spring follows winter. The days become longer and warmer. Plants begin to grow, and many animals have babies.

◁ Summer is the warmest season. Flowers bloom, and fruits grow in the sunshine. It does not get dark until late.

◁ In the fall, the days get shorter. The weather turns cooler. Trees may lose their leaves. Some birds fly to warmer places.

△ It is always hot near the equator. Often there is a dry season and a rainy season.

◁ Winter is the coldest season. It gets dark early in the evening. Plants stop growing, and many trees are bare.

Find out more

Antarctica and the Arctic

Birds

Plants

Trees

Weather

Ships and boats

Boats have been used for thousands of years to carry people and goods across water. The first boats were rafts, made from logs or reeds tied together. Boats use sails, oars, or engines to push them through the water. Large seagoing boats are called ships. There are many different types of ships and boats.

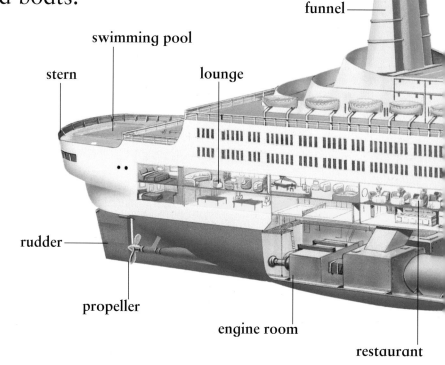

△ Long ago, the peoples of Polynesia explored the Pacific Ocean in boats like large canoes. They were searching for new islands.

▷ Huge passenger ships are called ocean liners or cruise ships. They are like floating hotels. The parts of a ship all have names. The front is called the bow, and the back is called the stern.

funnel

swimming pool

stern

lounge

rudder

propeller

engine room

restaurant

Viking longboat

△ The Vikings were great sailors. They built strong, wooden ships called longboats, which had square sails. They could also row their ships through the water with oars.

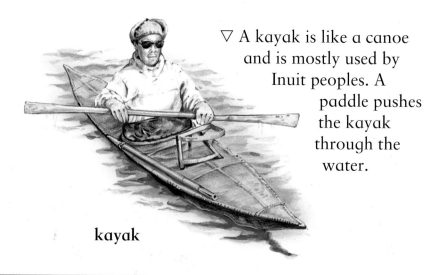

▽ A kayak is like a canoe and is mostly used by Inuit peoples. A paddle pushes the kayak through the water.

kayak

▷ A speedboat has a powerful engine. The front lifts up so that it can skim quickly across the top of the water.

speedboat

▽ A racing yacht has a large sail at the front called a spinnaker. When it catches the wind, the yacht races across the sea.

racing yacht

mast

bridge

bow

hull

movie theater

cabin

cruise ship

hull

▷ The biggest ships in the world are oil tankers. They can be 1,600 feet (500m) long and so heavy that they take 20 minutes to come to a stop.

water line

oil tanker

Find out more

Conservation
Fishing
History
Religion
Science
South America

Soil

The soil beneath your feet is made up of tiny bits of rock mixed with tiny pieces of plants. It is full of life. Hundreds of beetles, worms, slugs, and other even smaller things live there. Plants get water and the other important things that they need in order to grow from the soil.

Always wash your hands after you have played with soil.

△ After you shake soil in a jar of water, it will slowly settle into layers. Each layer is different. This shows you how many things make up soil.

soil after two days

▽ Many animals live in the ground. The roots of trees and grass stop the soil from being blown or washed away.

Worms tunnel into the soil.

Rabbits live in warrens.

Moles leave mounds above their homes.

Roots hold trees firmly in the ground.

Soil is made of sand, mud, stones, and dead plants.

Find out more
Farming
Mammals
Plants

Sound

Sounds are made when something vibrates. Vibration is when something moves back and forth very quickly. Sound is invisible and moves in waves through the air. Sound waves can also travel through a liquid, such as water, or a solid, such as glass.

Concorde

△ The Concorde could travel faster than the speed of sound. Its last flight was in 2003.

sound waves
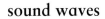

△ You hear sounds when sound waves reach your ears. Inside each ear you have an eardrum. Sound waves hit your eardrums and make them vibrate.

▷ When something vibrates very fast, like this whistle, it makes a high sound. Things that vibrate more slowly, such as this double bass, make a lower sound.

whistle

double bass

Find out more

Energy

Flying machines

Human body

Inventions

Music

123

South America

South America is the fourth-largest continent. It has hot and cold deserts and large, grassy plains. Down one side runs a long line of mountains called the Andes. The world's largest rainforest grows around the Amazon River. Many people in South America live in crowded cities and are very poor.

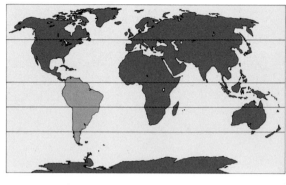

△ South America is shown in purple. It is joined to North America by a thin stretch of land called Central America.

▷ The people who live around Lake Titicaca, high up in the Andes Mountains, build their boats and houses out of reeds.

◁ Statues and ruins are all that is left of the ancient cities of South America. This statue is from a city called Tiahuanaco (tee-ah-**wa**-nah-**ko**).

▷ People raise llamas for their meat and wool. Llamas also carry heavy goods.

▷ Cowboys, called gauchos, care for enormous herds of cattle on the grassy plains of Argentina. These grasslands are called the Pampas.

▽ Angel Falls, in the rainforest of Venezuela, is the highest waterfall in the world.

▷ Macaws live in the lush Amazon rainforest. Snakes, monkeys, and big cats also live there.

scarlet macaw

◁ Rio de Janeiro is the main port of Brazil. A huge statue of Jesus Christ on Corcovado Mountain stands high up above Rio's beautiful bay.

Find out more
Conservation
Grasslands
World

125

Space exploration

To find out more about the planets and stars, scientists send rockets carrying people and objects into space. People who travel into space are called astronauts. They wear special suits in space to survive. Spacecraft are machines that can travel into space. One of the best known is the space shuttle. It was taken out of service in 2011.

▽ The space shuttle could carry up to seven astronauts into space. Its doors opened up in space to release its cargo of scientific instruments. An astronaut controlled a robot arm to move the cargo.

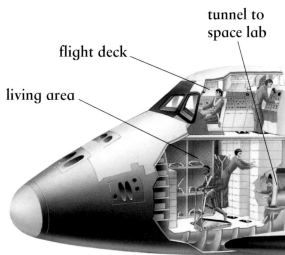

tunnel to space lab

flight deck

living area

Saturn V

◁ The biggest rocket ever built was called *Saturn V*. It carried the first astronauts to the Moon in 1969.

radio

air supply

helmet

◁ There is no air to breathe in space. Astronauts wear space suits for protection in order to work outside their spacecraft.

NASA

glove

space suit

boot

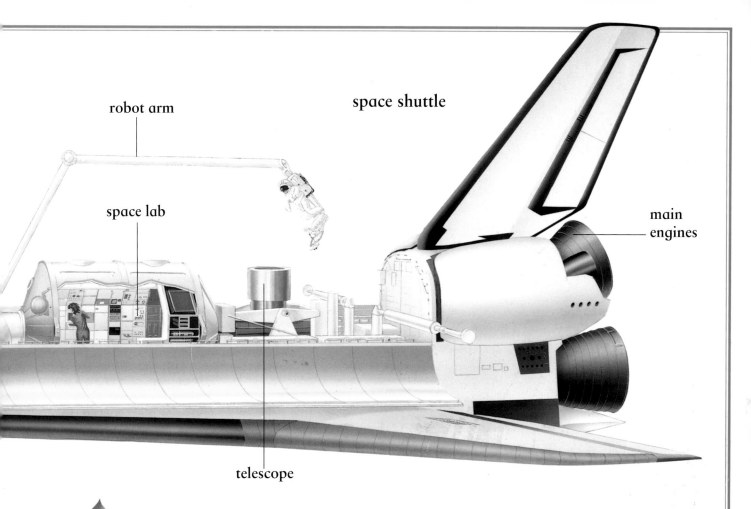

robot arm

space shuttle

space lab

main engines

telescope

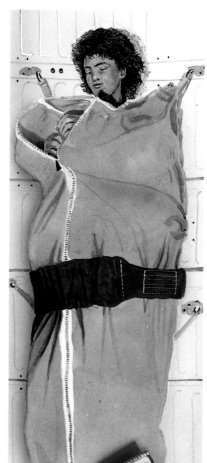

◁ The space shuttle took off with a huge fuel tank and two solid rocket boosters to blast it into space. It took only a few minutes for it to reach space.

solid rocket booster

◁ In space, nothing has any weight. Astronauts have to move around carefully. They are strapped into their sleeping bags to stop them from floating around.

Satellites and probes

Rockets also carry satellites and probes into space. These machines send back information to Earth.

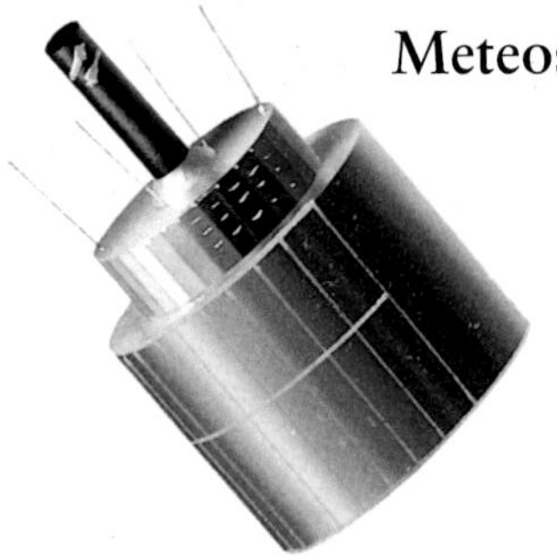

Meteosat

▷ The giant Hubble Space Telescope sends back pictures of stars and galaxies to astronomers on Earth.

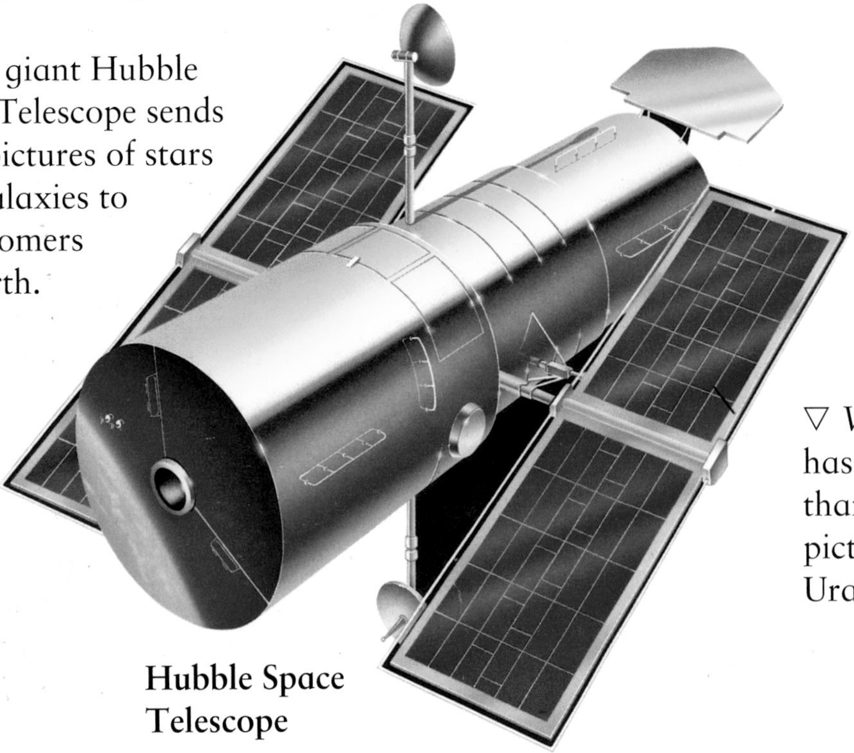

△ Meteosat watches weather patterns. It sends information to computers on Earth.

Hubble Space Telescope

▽ *Voyager 2* is a probe that has been in space for more than 30 years. It has sent back pictures of Jupiter, Saturn, Uranus, and Neptune.

Voyager 2

◁ These astronauts are fixing a broken satellite. The satellite has been taken into the space shuttle's repair bay.

Find out more
Inventions
Moon
Universe

Spiders

bird-eating spider

Spiders have eight legs. Insects are their main food. Most spiders spin sticky webs of silk to trap their prey. Some go hunting or lie waiting for prey to pass by. Spiders kill their prey by biting them with poisonous fangs.

△ This bird-eating spider has a leg span of 1 foot (3m) and lives in the South American rainforest. It sometimes catches birds in nests, but it usually eats insects that it hunts at night.

◁ The orb weaver feels movement in the web and knows that the dragonfly is struggling to escape. The spider rushes out to wrap its prey in silk and adds it to its supply of food.

orb weaver spider

trapdoor spider

dragonfly

◁ The trapdoor spider hunts by hiding behind a trapdoor in its burrow. When an insect is outside, the spider jumps out and pounces on it.

Find out more
Forests
Stories

129

Sports

People play sports for many reasons. It may be their job, or they may do it just for fun. Being active helps them stay strong and healthy. Some sports are played by one person. Others are played by two or more people. In many sports, two teams compete with each other. Some sports, such as horse racing, involve animals as well as people.

△ Soccer is played all over the world. In some countries it is called football. Players need great skill to control the ball with their feet.

▷ Baseball can be played at all ages. This young pitcher is developing his skills in a Little League game.

◁ Gymnasts start learning when they are very young. They practice how to perform difficult exercises on the floor and on special pieces of equipment—like this one, called the balance beam.

◁ In Mongolia, boys and girls as young as five dress up to take part in horse races.

▷ Hockey is one of the most popular North American sports. It is a fast and tough game. Players wear helmets and pads for protection.

▽ When two people play tennis against each other, it is called singles. When four play, it is called doubles.

△ Swimmers train hard to swim well and fast. They learn different strokes, called the breaststroke, backstroke, crawl, and butterfly.

▷ The Olympic Games is held every four years. Countries send their best athletes to compete.

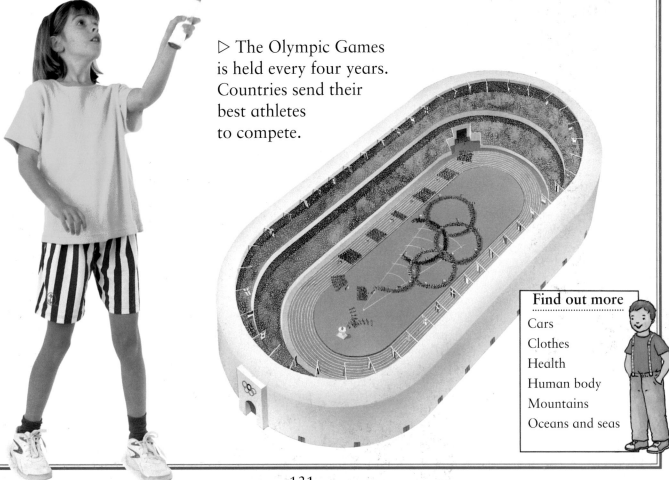

Find out more

Cars
Clothes
Health
Human body
Mountains
Oceans and seas

Stories

Stories tell you about events. Some stories are about real things, and others are made up. Long ago, people told one another stories about their gods or about real people who had done amazing things. Now we read stories in books and magazines or watch them in movies and on television.

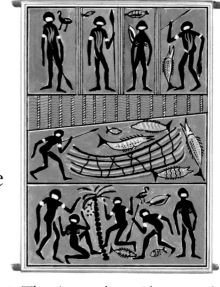

△ The Australian Aboriginal people paint stories of how they believe the land was made.

▽ Use your imagination to write your own story. Make it a scary, funny, or magical story. Draw pictures of the characters. Show what they did.

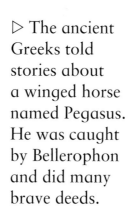

▷ The ancient Greeks told stories about a winged horse named Pegasus. He was caught by Bellerophon and did many brave deeds.

◁ In Africa, the Ashanti people, who live in Ghana, tell stories about a spider called Anansi who likes to play tricks.

▷ Comic strips tell stories with pictures. The words people say are written in speech bubbles.

▷ "Jack and the Beanstalk" is a folktale. Jack climbs up a huge beanstalk to steal a magic hen from a wicked and cruel giant.

◁ The story of *The Wizard of Oz* was made into a famous movie. Dorothy helps a scarecrow, a cowardly lion, and a tin man.

Find out more
Africa
Art and artists
Books
Dance
Drama

Sun

The Sun is a star. It is a dazzling ball of burning gases. The Sun is the closest, most important star to Earth. It gives us light and warmth. Earth is almost 93 million miles (149.5 million km) from the Sun. If Earth was closer, it would burn up. If it was farther away, it would be freezing cold.

△ During an eclipse, the Moon hides the Sun. This is the only time that we can see the clouds of white gas, called the corona, that surround the Sun.

Never look directly at the Sun. It could damage your eyes.

core

Prominences are jets of hot gas.

Sunspots are the coolest parts of the Sun.

Find out more
Earth
Energy
Light
Planets
Plants
Seashores
Seasons
Universe
Weather

Time

We use clocks and watches to measure time exactly in hours, minutes, and seconds. In the ancient past, people measured time roughly in days, nights, and seasons. Later people used shadow clocks, candle clocks, and sundials. At sea they used sand clocks such as the hourglass.

candle clock

◁ Candle clocks were marked in sections. The candle burned away one section every hour. People could tell the time by the number of sections left.

oven

△ Some ovens have a digital timer so that the oven can start or finish at a preset time.

alarm clock

△ An alarm clock can be set to wake you up in time for something. Many children use alarm clocks to wake them up in time for school.

stopwatch

△ This boy uses a stopwatch to time his friend, who is running a race. He stops the watch when his friend crosses the finish line.

Find out more

Earth
Machines
Moon
Seasons
Years

Trains

All over the world, trains pull heavy loads along rails. The rails make it easier for the wheels to turn. The first trains used steam engines to drive the wheels. Now most trains run on electricity or diesel fuel. Trains carry people and goods long distances at high speeds.

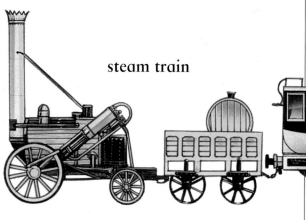

steam train

△ Steam trains were invented more than 200 years ago. They used coal or wood to make steam to drive the wheels.

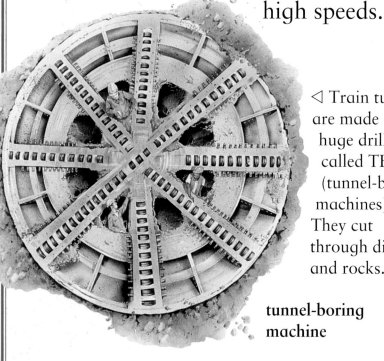

◁ Train tunnels are made by huge drills called TBMs (tunnel-boring machines). They cut through dirt and rocks.

tunnel-boring machine

△ Cities such as New York City, Boston, and San Francisco have subway systems. They run under the grouned on electrically charged rails.

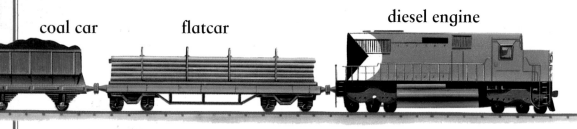

coal car   flatcar   diesel engine

◁ Trains that carry goods are called freight trains. Some can pull more than 100 cars.

◁ Some modern trains can travel very quickly. The fastest passenger train in the world can travel up to 250 miles per hour (400km/h).

Find out more
Electricity
Inventions
Machines

136

Trees

Trees are plants. They are among the largest living things on Earth. Many of them live for hundreds of years.

Trees give food and shelter to birds, insects, and many other animals. Mushrooms and other fungi grow on their roots and on dead tree stumps.

△ Each year a layer of wood grows inside the trunk of a tree and makes a ring. You can tell the age of a tree by counting the number of rings on the trunk.

deciduous

evergreen

maple samara

maple leaf

oak tree

acorn

oak leaf

spruce cone

monkey puzzle cones

spruce tree

△ Deciduous trees start to lose their leaves in the fall and have no leaves in the winter. They grow new leaves in the spring.

△ Evergreen trees keep their leaves all year long. Many have spiky, needlelike leaves that are not harmed by the cold.

Find out more

Conservation
Flowers
Forests
Mountains
Plants
Prehistoric life
Seasons
Soil

Trucks

Trucks are built to carry all types of things. They take food and other goods from farms and factories to stores. They carry all of your furniture and possessions when you move to a new house. They are built to be very strong and can travel long distances—even from one end of the country to the other.

△ This truck is called a road train. Road trains can pull three huge trailers. They are used in Australia.

△ The crane on the back of a logging truck is used to lift logs onto the trailer. This truck is used in places with large forests.

trailer

trailer hook

mirror

tractor unit

▷ This truck is a tractor-trailer. It has two parts. A trailer is hooked onto a cab called a tractor by a hinge. This helps it go around sharp curves.

fuel tank

light

◁ Small pickup trucks may have open backs. They are useful for short-distance transportation.

Find out more
Conservation
Machines
Roads

Universe

The universe contains light and energy and all living things. It is very hard to imagine how big the universe really is. Earth, the Sun, the other planets, and all of the stars that you can see in the sky at night make up our galaxy, called the Milky Way. Some people talk about the Milky Way galaxy as being the universe, but it is only one tiny part of the whole universe. There are many galaxies in the universe.

△ Even when you look through a telescope, you can see only a tiny part of the universe.

◁ This picture is of huge groups of stars called galaxies. It was taken in space by the Hubble Space Telescope.

Hubble Space Telescope

The life of a star

New stars are being made all the time. They shine for a very long time, and then they die. A red giant is a huge, old star.

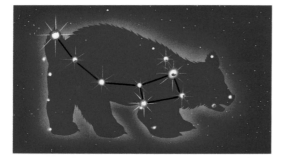

Little Dipper

Southern Cross

△ Long ago, people gave names to patterns made by stars in the sky. These patterns are called constellations. The Little Dipper can be seen by people living in the northern part of the world. The Southern Cross can be seen by people living in the southern part.

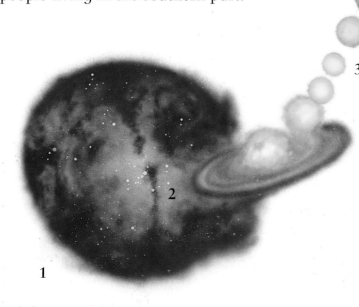

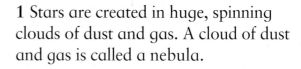

3

1 Stars are created in huge, spinning clouds of dust and gas. A cloud of dust and gas is called a nebula.

2 The gas and dust shrink and join to form many balls. These become a cluster of baby stars.

3 As a star gets hotter, it begins to shine. Most stars, including our Sun, shine steadily during almost all of their lives.

1

2

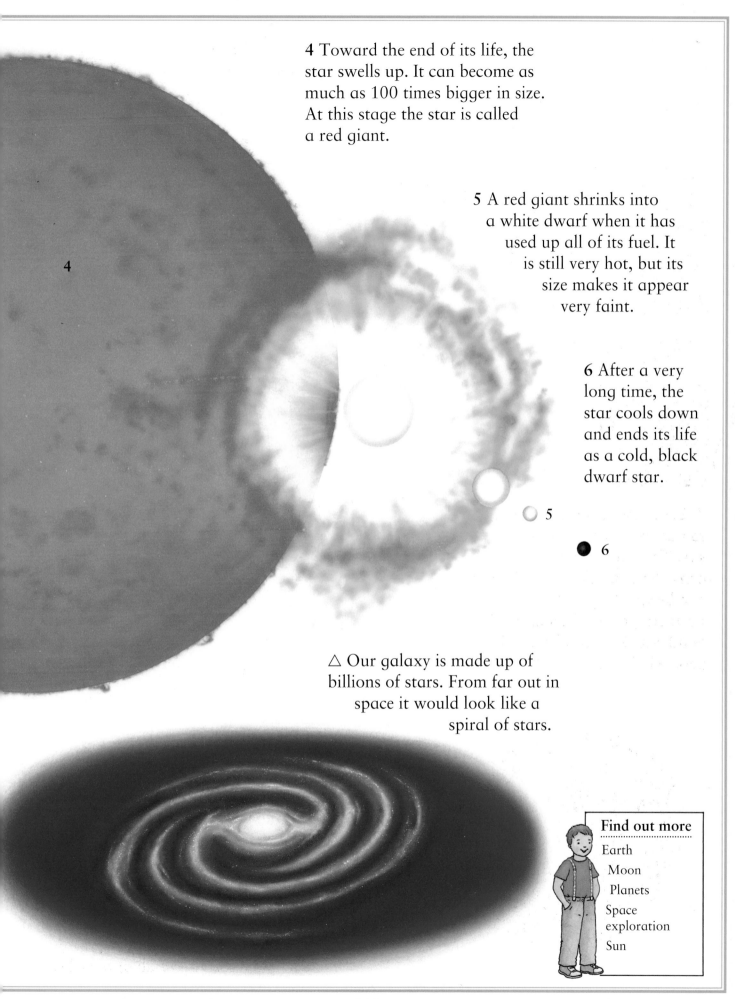

4 Toward the end of its life, the star swells up. It can become as much as 100 times bigger in size. At this stage the star is called a red giant.

5 A red giant shrinks into a white dwarf when it has used up all of its fuel. It is still very hot, but its size makes it appear very faint.

6 After a very long time, the star cools down and ends its life as a cold, black dwarf star.

4

5

6

△ Our galaxy is made up of billions of stars. From far out in space it would look like a spiral of stars.

Find out more

Earth

Moon

Planets

Space exploration

Sun

Volcanoes

A volcano is a mountain made of ash and hot, runny rock called lava. Ash, lava, and gas spurt out of a crack in Earth's surface. When the lava cools, it hardens into rock. Volcanoes may erupt once and then not again for many years.

lava

Find out more
Earth
Oceans and seas

Water

water strider

All life on Earth needs water. Without it, everything would die. Water covers almost three fourths of the world. There is salt water in the oceans and seas and fresh water in lakes, rivers, and ponds. Ice, or frozen water, usually covers the oceans around Antarctica and the Arctic. All of these watery places are home to many different plants and animals.

△ A water strider can walk on water because of a force called surface tension. This force makes a thin, stretchy layer on the water.

▷ When water is a liquid, it flows and spreads. When it is poured into a container, it has a flat surface.

▷ If water becomes very cold, it freezes and turns into solid ice. When ice melts, it turns back into water.

ice

water

▽ When steam hits something cold, it cools and turns into water droplets. This change is called condensation.

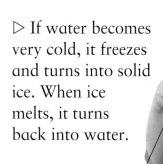

▽When water is very hot, it boils. Bubbles rise up, burst, and release steam.

steam

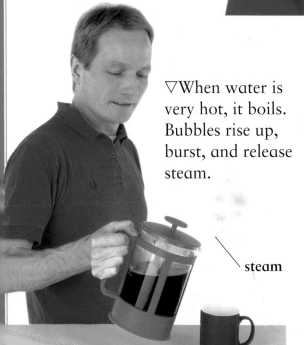

condensation

143

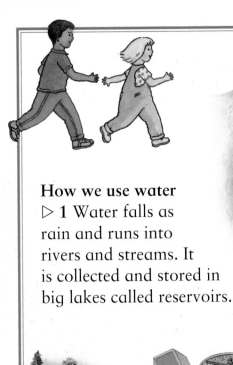

How we use water
▷ **1** Water falls as rain and runs into rivers and streams. It is collected and stored in big lakes called reservoirs.

▷ **2** The water is cleaned.

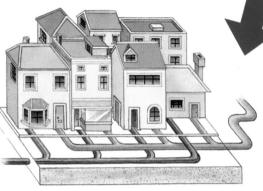

▽ **3** Water is pumped through pipes into houses.

△ **5** The water is cleaned. Then it flows back into a river or the ocean.

△ **4** After it has been used, the water goes down through drainpipes into sewers.

▽ Plants need water. Their roots soak up water from the soil. The water travels up the stems to the leaves, where it helps make food.

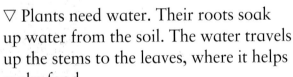

Fact box
• You lose water from your body when you sweat, breathe, and go to the bathroom.
• You need to drink around 1.6 quarts (1.5L) of water per day to stay healthy.
• You could not live for more than three days without water.

◁ More than two thirds of your body is made of water.

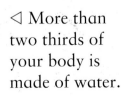

◁ In the dry savanna of Africa, groups of animals gather at a watering hole. As they take a long drink, they watch out for hungry lions.

▽ This mangrove swamp is a wet area of land near the ocean. Mangrove trees have long, strong roots to anchor them in the mud.

◁ A salmon swims from the ocean in order to lay its eggs in the river where it was born. Some bears wait near waterfalls to catch salmon.

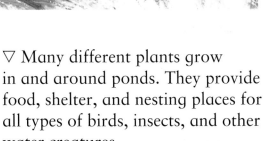

▽ Many different plants grow in and around ponds. They provide food, shelter, and nesting places for all types of birds, insects, and other water creatures.

Find out more

Amphibians
Animals
Caves
Energy
Fish
Oceans and seas
Plants
Science
Seashores
Weather
World

Weather

Three things cause the weather: air, sunlight, and water. Air is always moving and creates wind. Sunlight gives warmth, and water makes clouds, rain, snow, and hail. In some parts of the world, the weather changes all the time. One day the sky may be sunny, and the next day it may be cloudy.

▽ This picture shows how Earth uses its water over and over again. This is called the **water cycle**.

1 Every day the Sun's heat turns water from oceans and lakes into an invisible gas called water vapor.

2 As the air rises, it cools down, and the water vapor turns into tiny droplets of water or ice crystals.

3 Many droplets of water join together to form clouds. The wind blows the clouds over the land.

4 Water in the clouds falls as rain, hail, sleet, or snow.

5 Rivers carry the water back to the ocean.

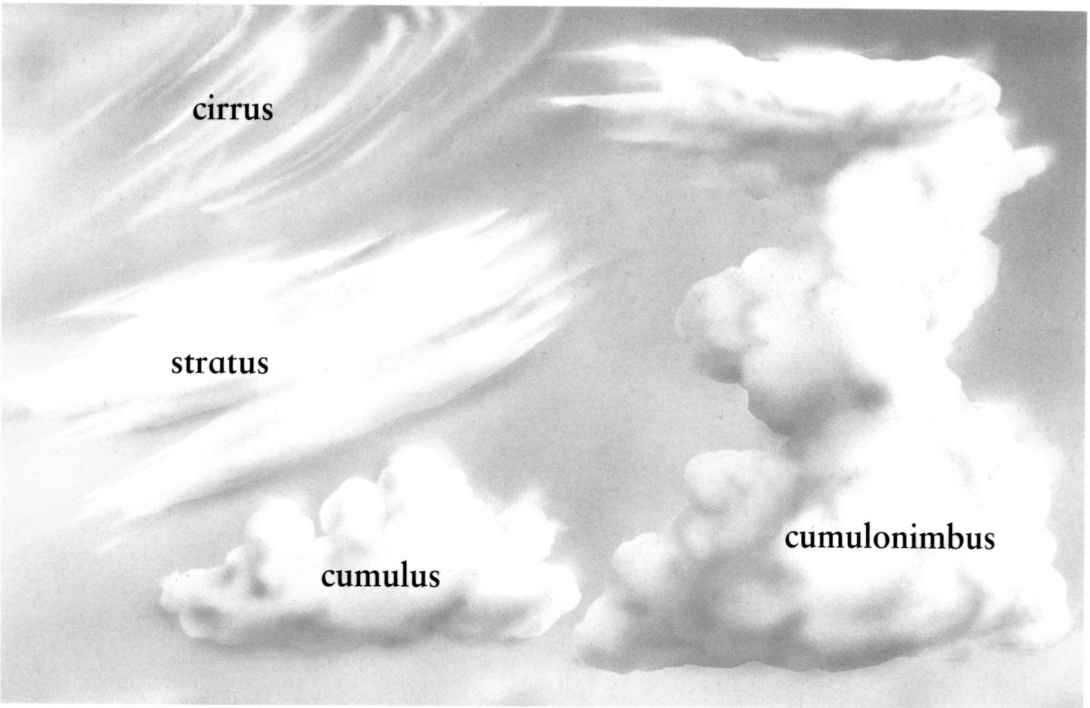

cirrus

stratus

cumulus

cumulonimbus

◁ There are different types of clouds. Fluffy clouds are called cumulus. Flat clouds are called stratus. Huge cumulonimbus clouds bring storms. Cirrus clouds are high up and wispy.

▷ Snowflakes are water droplets that have frozen into ice crystals. No two snowflakes are ever the same.

▽ In very cold places, ice and snow often cover the land for most of the year.

△ Fog and mist are really clouds floating close to the ground. On roads, thick fog makes it difficult for drivers to see where they are going.

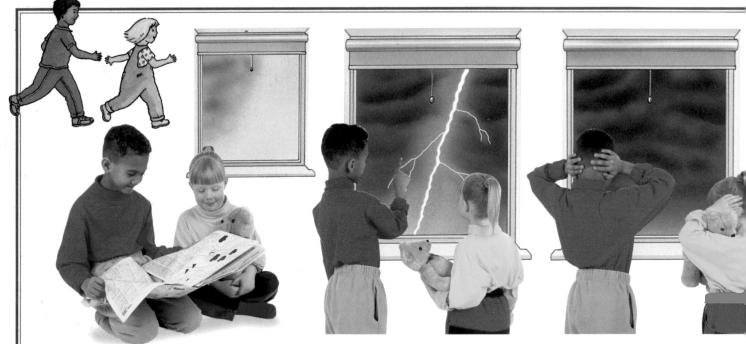

△ Thunderstorms start in big, black thunderclouds that gather in the sky.

△ Electricity builds up inside the clouds. This causes big sparks of lightning.

△ When lightning flashes, it heats the air and makes a noise. This is thunder.

◁ A tornado is a spinning funnel of wind that races across the ground. As it spins, it sucks up rocks, trees, and even houses in its path.

△ Hailstones are frozen drops of rain. As they blow around inside a cloud, layers of ice form around them until they are heavy enough to fall.

barometer

thermometer

△ A barometer is an instrument that is used to measure the pressure of the air. If the air pressure changes, it usually means that there will be a change in the weather.

▷ A thermometer is an instrument that is used to measure the temperature of the air. This shows how hot or how cold it is outside.

weathervane

△ A weathervane shows in which direction the wind is blowing. Winds that blow from the west are called westerlies. Winds that blow from the north are called northerlies.

◁ A rain gauge is used to measure rainfall. The rain falls through a funnel into a container. A scale shows how much rain has fallen.

rain gauge

Find out more

Air
Clothes
Earth
Energy
Light
Seasons
Space
exploration
Sun
Water

World

Oceans cover most of the world. Around one third of the world is covered by land. There are seven large areas of land called continents. People have divided most of them into countries. Each country has its own name, its own government, and its own flag. There are around 190 countries in the world. Many different peoples live in each one.

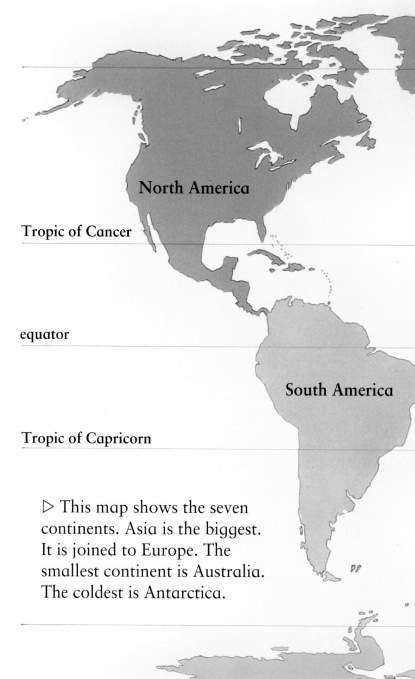

North America

Tropic of Cancer

equator

South America

Tropic of Capricorn

▷ This map shows the seven continents. Asia is the biggest. It is joined to Europe. The smallest continent is Australia. The coldest is Antarctica.

▽ On globes and maps, an imaginary line called the equator divides the world in half. Countries closest to the equator are the hottest.

globe

▷ The world is round. To draw a flat map of it, mapmakers sometimes split its surface into several pieces, as if peeling an orange.

equator

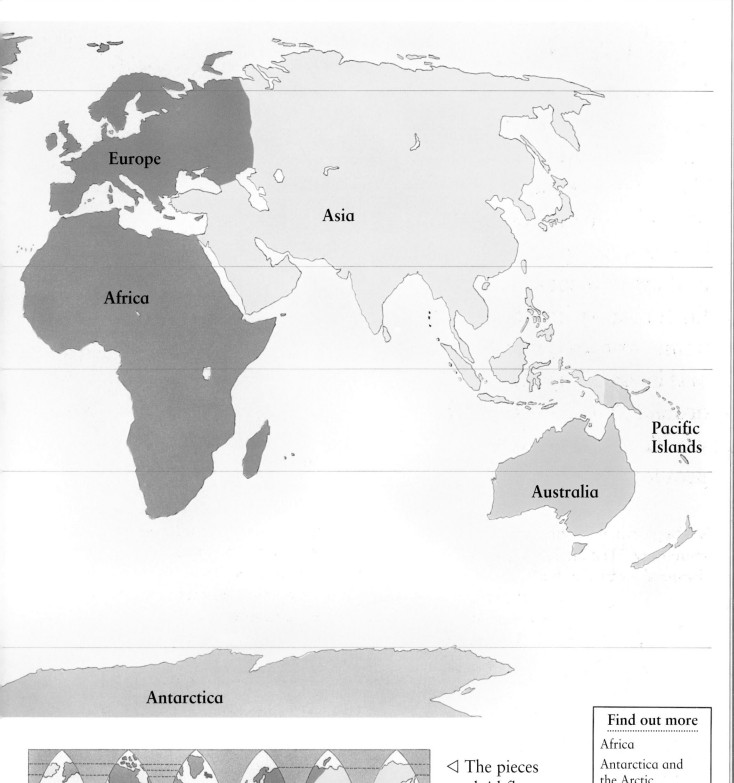

Europe

Asia

Africa

Pacific
Islands

Australia

Antarctica

◁ The pieces
are laid flat
like this. But
no flat map
can show us
that the world
has a curved
surface.

equator

Writing

Writing is very useful. It is a way of marking down words and ideas so that people can read them. Writing may be made up of small pictures or signs. Another type of writing may be made up of letters of an alphabet. Each letter stands for one sound. Joining the letters together makes words.

△ This writing is on baked tablets of clay. It tells us what was in the storeroom of a Greek palace, including weapons and chariot wheels.

नमस्ते
Hindi

Здравствуйте
Russian

מרחבاً
Arabic

שלום
Hebrew

你好
Mandarin

△ This is how "hello" is written in several different languages. Each one uses its own special alphabet.

△ You use words to write letters, messages, lists, and stories. Writing helps you remember and share your thoughts and ideas.

▷ Blind people can read by touching groups of raised dots. Each letter is a different pattern of dots. This is known as Braille.

Find out more

Books
Stories

X-rays

X-rays are invisible beams that help us take pictures of things that we cannot see through. Dentists and doctors use X-rays to look at our teeth and inside our bodies. These pictures are also called X-rays. Bones show up very clearly on an X-ray. X-ray machines at airports can see through bags to check what is inside them.

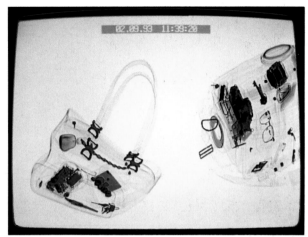

△ At the airport, luggage is put through an X-ray machine to check for metal weapons. Any guns or knives show up on the screen.

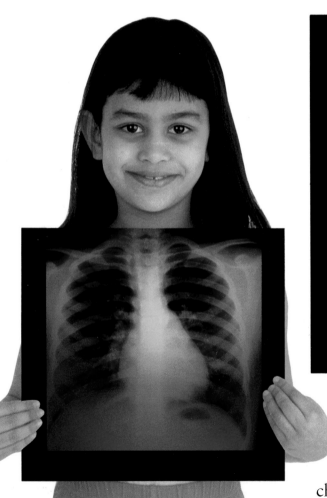

broken bone

◁ Doctors use X-rays to find out if a bone is broken. They are careful to use X-rays only when necessary because too many are not good for you.

◁ This X-ray picture shows the inside of this girl's chest. X-rays cannot pass through bones, so the bones show up as white shadows.

Find out more
Human body
Light

153

Years

A year is a length of time. Each year has 365 days. The days are divided into 12 months. Every four years an extra day is added. This is called a leap year. Throughout the year, celebrations take place all over the world. Some are to remember things that have happened during a country's history or to celebrate the changing of the seasons.

△ All over the United States, people celebrate Independence Day on July 4 with parades, marching bands, picnics, pageants, and fireworks.

▷ Chinese New Year is celebrated between January and February. People dress up and set off noisy firecrackers in the street.

▽ Birthday parties are a popular way to celebrate the day someone was born. Which day is your birthday?

Find out more
Babies
Moon
Seasons

Zoos

Zoos are places where wild animals are kept so that people can learn about them. Many zoos keep animals in big, open areas with plenty of space. They protect and breed animals that are in danger of dying out.

△ Once there were no Père David's deer alive in the wild. Luckily, zoos bred them successfully, and they now live on the grasslands of China.

▽ Pandas are becoming more rare in the wild. A few live in zoos, where everyone hopes they will breed.

◁ Tamarin monkeys live in the rainforests of Brazil. In a good zoo, animals live in areas like their homes in the wild.

Find out more
Animals
Conservation

155

Glossary

A **glossary** is a list of useful words. Some of the words used in this book may be new to you, and so they are explained again here.

Aboriginal people The first people to live in a country. This term usually refers to Australian Aboriginal people.

ancestor A person who lived in your family before you.

arteries and **veins** Arteries are tubes inside the human body that carry blood away from the heart, and veins are tubes that carry blood toward it.

atmosphere The layer of air that surrounds Earth. It contains the oxygen we breathe and protects us from the Sun's dangerous rays.

billion One thousand million.

border The line where one country ends and another country begins.

capital city A country's most important city. It is usually the city from which the government rules.

chrysalis The stage in the life cycle of a butterfly or moth between the adult and caterpillar stages.

conifer A tree, such as a pine or fir, that carries its seeds in cones.

continent One of the seven large areas of land. They are: Africa, Antarctica, Asia, Australia, Europe, North America, and South America.

deciduous Describes a tree that loses all of its leaves once a year in the fall.

effort and **force** Effort is the work done to move something. A force pushes or pulls an object in a specific direction.

evergreen A tree that has leaves on it all year long.

generator A machine used to make electricity.

hibernation When an animal sleeps through the winter.

migration When an animal moves from one place to another each year.

mineral Any natural material found in the ground that does not come from a plant or an animal.

orbit The curved path of an object that travels around a star or a planet.

oxygen A type of gas found in air. We need to breathe in oxygen in order to live. Our bodies use oxygen and food to make energy.

pole The most northern and southern points on Earth. Each end of a magnet is also called a pole.

prehistoric Describes a very long time ago, before human history was written down.

prey Animals that are hunted and killed by other animals for food.

static electricity Electricity that does not run along wires in a steady current. Lightning is static electricity. It happens when electricity builds up in clouds and then leaps to the ground. Rubbing a balloon on a sweater makes static electricity.

submersible A small submarine, used especially for underwater exploration.

vibration When something moves back and forth very quickly.

water vapor Water is usually a liquid, but it can also be a solid (called ice) or a gas (called water vapor).

Index

This index helps you find the subjects in this book. It is in alphabetical order. Main entries are in **bold,** or **dark,** letters. This is where you will find the most information on your subject.

The Publisher would like to thank the following for contributing to this book:

Photographs

Page **6** Spectrum Colour Library; **7** Spectrum Colour Library *t*, Planet Earth Pictures *m*; **15** NHPA *t*, Brian and Cherry Alexander *bl*, TRIP *m*; **16** Bridgeman Art Library *l*, Archiv für Kunst und Geschichte *b*; **17** © ARS, NY and DACS, London 1996 *b*, Bridgeman Art Library *tr*; **19** NHPL; **20** Lawson Woods; **21** Images *t*, Spectrum Colour Library *b*; **22** Robert Harding *l*, Lupe Cunha Pictures *r*; **36** Science Museum/Science and Society Picture Library; **37** Trip *t*, Science Photo Library *r*; **47** Natural History Museum; **51** Telegraph Colour Library *t*, Image Select *r*; **53** Zefa *t*, Spectrum Colour Library *b*; **60** Mary Evans Picture Library; **70** Zefa *l*, Colorific *r*; **71** Spectrum Colour Library *t*, Image Select *r*; **72** Spectrum Colour Library *m*, Image Select *b*; **73** AKG Photo *t*, Greg Evans International *m*; **83** Hutchison Library *l*, Colorific *r*; **94** Zefa *l*, Telegraph Colour Library *b*; **95** Alamy, Corbis; **97** Zefa; **100** Dognall Worldwide; **101** Images *r*, Colorific *l*; **102** Zefa; **98** Greg Evans International; **110** Rex Features; **111** Colorific; **112** Colorific *t*, Circa Photo Library *l*; **113** Telegraph Colour Library *ml*, TRIP *tr*; **122** Liam Muir *mr*; **125** Zefa *bl*, Cine Contact *t*; **130** Greg Evans International *l*, Allsport U.S.A. *r*; **131** Allsport; **133** Ronald Grant *b*, © 1996 Marvel Characters Inc. *m*; **139** Science Photo Library; **147** Zefa *m*, Zefa *r*; **148** Zefa; **152** Gilda Pacitti *b*; **153** Telegraph Colour Library *t*, Science Photo Library *b*
All other commissioned photographs Tim Ridley

Artists

Hemesh Alles, Craig Austin, Julian Baker, Bob Bampton, Julie Banyard, John Barber, Peter Barrett, Richard Bonson, Maggie Brand, Eric T. Budge, John Butler, Lynn Chadwick, Harry Clow, Stephen Conlin, David Cook, Bob Corley, Peter Dennis, Maggie Downer, Richard Draper, Michael Fisher, Eugene Fleury, Roy Flooks, Chris Forsey, Rosamund Fowler, Mark Franklin, Andrew French, Terry Gabbey, Michael Gaffrey, Lee Gibbons (Wildlife Art Agency), Tony Gibbons, Mike Gillah, Peter Goodfellow, Ruby Green, Craig Greenwood, Peter Gregory, Ray Grinaway, J. Haysom, Tim Hayward (Bernard Thornton Artists), Steven Holmes, Adam Hook, Christa Hook, Biz Hull, Mark Iley, Ian Jackson, Ron Jobson (Kathy Jakeman), Kevin Jones, B. L. Kearley, Roger Kent (Garden Studio), Deborah Kindred, Mike Lacey, Stuart Lafford, Terence Lambert, R. Lewington, Bernard Long (Temple Rogers), S. McAllinson, Angus McBride, Doreen McGuinness (Garden Studio), B. McIntyre, Kevin Maddison (Mainline Design), Alan Male (Linden Artists), Shirley Mallinson, Maltings Partnership, Janos Marffy, David Marshall (Simon Girling and Associates), Josephine Martin, Tony Morris (Maggie Mundy Illustrators Agency), Steve Noon (Oxford Illustrators), Nicki Palin, Alex Pang, Darren Pattenden, Bruce Pearson, Clive Pritchard, Sebastian Quigley (Linden Artists), Elizabeth Rice, J. Rignall, Bernard Robinson, Eric Robson, Eric Rowe, Liz Sawyer, Brian Smith, Guy Smith (Mainline), Annabel Spencely, Clive Spong, Paul Stangroom, Roger Stewart, Treve Tamblin, Myke Taylor (Garden Studios), Simon Tegg, Ian Thompson, Ross Watton, Graham White, Ann Winterbotham, David Wright

Models

Afua Arhin, Akua Arhin, Kirsty Bailey, Jack Clements, Sheila Clewley, Ceci Cole, Christopher Davis, James Fenwick, Hugo Flaux, Laurie Flaux, Toby Flaux, Ella Fraser, Olivia Gardner, Jessie Grisewood, John Grisewood, Katie Hill, Lucy Hill, Flora Kent, Josh Kent, Alexander Kendall, Fay Killick, Mia Mackinnon, Emma Makinson, Lucy Makinson, Hannah Mitchell, Georgina Ratnatunga, Louis Robertson, James Sullivan, Claire Tolman, Nicholas Tolman, Tom Whittington

Scallywags:
Gemma Loke, Meera Patel, Dwayne Thomas, Ahmani Vidal-Simon, David Watts, Jordan White

Tiny Tots to Teens:
Lauren Charles, Ken King, Jose Oliveira

Truly Scrumptious Ltd.:
Nicholas Loblack, Tara Saddiq, Milo Taylor